SUPER BOWL HEROES

by Stu Black

Watermill Press

CONTENTS

BART STARR—
SUPER BOWL I

As the Green Bay Packers' quarterback in the 1960s, Bart Starr became one of the best signal-callers in pro football and led his team to two Super Bowl wins. He played under Coach Vince Lombardi, a tough man but one of the greatest coaches in football history. A quiet player, Starr was the exact opposite of his boss, yet he was the man who carried out Lombardi's orders on the field. Starr was as reliable as the sun rising in the east and setting in the west.

Bart Starr's personal qualities are as memorable as his ability to throw a football. Soon after he led the Green Bay Packers to a second Super Bowl victory, Starr was named one of the "Ten Most Outstanding Young Men In The United States." Why had Starr been so honored? Because on the field or off, he showed leadership, courage, and the ability to handle any situation.

Though he was soft-spoken, Bart was still a firm leader. He accepted his teammates' mistakes as long as they gave their best. He only got upset if they failed because they didn't try. Bart felt, since he always gave his best, every other player should, too.

1

When Bart first joined the Packers, he was shy and not very confident of his abilities.

"He spent more time looking at his own shoes than other people's eyes," a writer noticed. "Hard guys around the league took advantage of him."

Then one day Bill George, a rough linebacker for the Chicago Bears, charged in and punched him in the mouth.

"That'll take care of you," George snarled.

Suddenly Bart got very angry. He realized that, because of his good nature, he had allowed this kind of rough stuff to go for too long. He had finally had it. Bart challenged George to a fight even though George was 40 pounds heavier! Players on both teams jumped between them before a punch was thrown, but it was finally clear that Bart Starr would stand up for his rights.

The Packers won two straight world championships when Bart Starr was their quarterback, but he was often the forgotten man. In the locker room, writers would chase Paul Hornung and Jim Taylor and Ray Nitschke while missing Bart. Because of his low-key personality, Bart was not colorful or flamboyant. But as former quarterback great Norm Van Brocklin often said, "The toughest part about playing quarterback is winning." With Bart Starr at quarterback, the Packers won.

Vince Lombardi is a Hall of Fame coach. He won that honor because he believed very strongly about certain things. One of the things he believed was that a quarterback meant everything to an offensive unit. Obviously, he felt that way about Bart Starr.

"Out of the 65 or 70 plays we run in a game," Lombardi once wrote, "I don't send in more than ten. Bart is great at picking a defense apart. He has a great memory, dedication and desire. He is also a great student of the game."

Early in his career, Bart was often accused of being too conservative in his play-calling. Some fans thought he should have been more daring. But they failed to realize that Bart was only following Lombardi's orders. The Packer system was conservative. They liked to play ball-control football—running plays and short passes. Lombardi liked old-fashioned, fundamental football. He thought the team that made the fewest mistakes won football games, and a basic, ball-control attack usually led to a minimum of errors. Later in Bart's career, many of the restrictions were removed from his play-calling and he became the master of the third-and-one fake run, long pass. Midway in the 1964 season, an imaginative call by Bart shocked Coach Lombardi.

The Packers were trailing the Cleveland Browns, 14-7, in the third quarter. They were on their own 44-yard line and needed less than a foot for a first down. The Browns brought in additional big linemen, assuming that Bart would give the ball to his powerful fullback, Jim Taylor, on a straight-ahead dive.

"We're going to cross them up," Bart said to split end Max McGee in the huddle. "I'm going to hit you over the middle." At the snap, Starr faked a hand-off to Taylor. The Browns' defensive linemen charged forward to stop the fullback. As the linemen and the fullback collided, Bart stepped back into his passing pocket, straightened up, and zipped the ball to McGee. McGee caught it and burst through the surprised Cleveland defenders. A saving tackle brought him down on the one-yard line, but seconds later the Packers scored the tying touchdown and went on to defeat the Browns, 28-21.

Bart possessed another trait which pleased Coach Lombardi. He played with what the Coach called "the small hurts." When Lombardi took over the Packers in 1959, he walked into the trainer's room on the second day of training camp and found half the squad lined up for treatment.

"What is this, a hospital?" Lombardi shouted. "Don't you men know you have to play with the small hurts?" He looked around the room slowly. His meaning was clear. If you couldn't play with the small hurts, you couldn't play for the Packers. The trainer's room emptied. After that, the Packers played with the small hurts.

During the 1961 season, Bart Starr played with a big hurt, a torn stomach muscle. He first suffered the injury in October, and week by week it grew worse. Eventually, he had trouble standing up straight enough to pass.

"Tell the coach about it," one of his teammates suggested. "This isn't a small hurt. This is a serious injury."

Bart refused. "The coach has enough troubles without worrying about me," he said. "I can play with it."

Starr played so well that the Packers lost only one of six games while he was injured. That year, they won their first league championship of the Lombardi era. When the Packers mailed out their contracts for the 1962 season, Starr looked at what he was offered and was very unhappy. He thought he deserved more money. The next morning, he went in to see Lombardi.

"Coach," the quarterback said to Lombardi, who doubled as general manager, "I'd have signed anything you gave me a couple of years ago. But you've taught me to be more aggressive and have more confidence in myself. So this is what I want," he said, naming a higher salary figure. Lombardi looked at him and chuckled.

"So that's it," Lombardi said. "Like Dr. Frankenstein, I've created a monster."

Starr smiled. His smile widened when Lombardi agreed to give him more money.

Bart Starr grew up on a military base in Montgomery, Alabama, where his father was a sergeant. Almost every evening, Bart's father would toss around either a football or baseball with Bart and his younger brother, Hilton. Bart was very close to his brother. They fought sometimes, the way brothers do, but mostly they played games together, fished together, or just roamed around having fun together. One day when Bart was 12 and Hilton was 10, they were playing "hide and seek," in their bare feet. Hilton stepped on a partially buried bone, and the bone punctured one of his feet. Although he received medical attention, the puncture led to a tetanus infection, and Hilton soon died. For many years after, Bart felt what he called "a real vacuum, an emptiness." He missed his brother terribly and thought about him often.

In 1974, Starr was introduced at a press conference as the Packers' new head coach.

When Bart entered high school in Montgomery, he went out for the football team, but didn't do very well. The coach told him that he hadn't made the first team and wasn't a good enough substitute to be on the squad that traveled to other schools for away games. If he wanted to, Bart was told, he could practice with the team and sit on the bench during home games, but that was all.

When Bart came home, he felt terrible, That night, he told his father he was quitting football. "Fine," said his father. "That will give you time to cut down those old cornstalks in the garden and turn over the earth for spring planting." More than anything else, Bart hated to work in the garden, so he continued to go to football practice.

Bart didn't play as a high-school sophomore or junior. He wasn't scheduled to play much as a senior either, but when the first-string quarterback broke his leg, Bart got a chance. He played so well that he won a football scholarship to the University of Alabama.

Through his first two years at the University, Bart maintained a straight-A average in his classes. In his sophomore year, he became the starting quarterback. He had shown the coaches in the last game of his freshman season that he could be a good quarterback when he led the Alabama "Crimson Tide" to a 61-6 victory in the Orange Bowl. In that game, Starr completed 8 out of 12 passes, as the Alabama team drove through Syracuse like a knife through butter. The following year, Alabama appeared in the Cotton Bowl, suffering a 28-6 loss. With the approach of his junior year, Bart's coach, Red Drew, looked forward to a successful season. Then Bart hurt his back while punting in practice. He strained muscles but kept on playing. Each time he played, he damaged his back further. When he finally went to a doctor, Bart was told he wouldn't be able to play football for quite a while. That season, Bart missed most of the Alabama schedule.

Bart was healthy again as a senior, but Alabama had hired a new coach, Ears Whitworth, who didn't want seniors on his starting team. He was looking to build strength for the future and chose to play sophomores and juniors so they could get experience under fire. Bart sat on the bench and watched less talented players than he lose all ten games that season. "Any confidence I had built up in the first 20 years of my life was almost shattered then," Bart said.

Because he hadn't played as a college senior, Bart wasn't high on any pro team's drafting list. In fact, his name didn't even appear on most lists. But his old coach, Red Drew, tipped off the Packers to Bart's potential, and Green Bay picked him as a 17th-round draft choice.

Bart joined the Packers in 1956, and for his first two years was the team's back-up quarterback. In 1958, the Packers traded their number-one quarterback, Tobin Rote. But just when Bart thought he was graduating to the number-one quarterback slot, Green Bay made one more trade and secured veteran quarterback Vito "Babe" Parelli. Babe had been an All-American quarterback at the University of Kentucky when Bart was in high school. In those days pictures of Parelli hung from every wall in Bart's room.

Bart fooled Packer management when he beat out his boyhood hero for the starting job. Then he got hurt and had to sit out much of the 1958 season. The next year, Vince Lombardi took over as coach and general manager. One of his first moves was to trade for a new quarterback. He acquired long-time Cardinal starter, Lamar McHan and gave him Bart's first-string job.

For most of that 1959 season, McHan was the starting quarterback. Unfortunately for him, the more Lombardi saw of his play, the less he liked it. Finally, the coach gave Bart a chance to run the team, and as the season ended, the Packers won four straight games. Pleased with Bart's progress, Lombardi named him the team's number-one quarterback for the 1960 season. The Packer dynasty came to full flower with Bart Starr at quarterback. Green Bay won the Western Conference championship in 1960, then won National Football League titles in 1961, 1962, 1965, 1966, and 1967. In the latter two years, they also won the first two Super Bowl games against American Football League competition.

In January 1967, the Green Bay Packers, representing the old line National Football League played the Kansas City Chiefs of the upstart American Football League in the first Super Bowl. The NFL, which had been in existence for nearly 50 years then, was putting its reputation on the line against the younger league, a mere seven years old. A defeat would make the older league look foolish. The NFL's champions, the Green Bay Packers, were expected to uphold the older league's pride and reputation against their hungry rivals.

Thirty-two-year-old Bart Starr carried much of the pressure placed on the Packers that day. He was the quarterback, and the quarterback always carries the major share of the responsibility. A curious nation watched the game that was played in the huge Los Angeles Coliseum on January 15, 1967.

Early on, the pressure on Starr increased mightily when it appeared that Kansas City might pull an upset. For the first two quarters, the Chiefs played the Packers fairly evenly, blunting their running attack, harassing Starr when he tried to throw, and moving the ball with consistency against the Packer defense. At half time, the Chiefs only trailed 14-10.

Then the game began to change. After the half-time break, Starr began to figure out where the Chiefs' defensive weak spots were. He began throwing passes to tight end Marv Fleming and wide receivers Carroll Dale and Max McGee. McGee caught the first touchdown pass on an inside pattern. The Kansas City cornerback that Bart thought might be his opponents' weak link, had dived frantically, trying to knock the pass away, and wound up lying helplessly on the turf. That one play confirmed Kansas City's fatal weakness.

The Packers scored again late in the third period as their running game, aided by Bart's passing, began to click. Mixing running and passing, Bart took the team down the field on a 56-yard drive. Three times he hit McGee in this series—once for 11 yards, once for 16, and once again for 13 yards and a touchdown. All three passes were the same: McGee beat the cornerback on a down-and-in pattern.

Lombardi had taught Bart that, when he found a weakness, he should exploit it endlessly.

Green Bay scored again in the fourth quarter. Bart's first pass to Dale moved the ball from the Green Bay 20-yard line to their 45. Another Starr-to-McGee pass covered 37 yards. After a running play failed to gain any yardage, Bart passed to Dale for seven yards. The ball rested on the Chiefs' 11. From there it was run-in for a touchdown.

When the dust cleared, the Packers had won the first Super Bowl convincingly, 35-10. For the time being, the NFL could go on feeling it was the superior league. As he did so often in important games, Bart played almost errorless ball against Kansas City. "Starr picks out a weak spot and stays with it better than any quarterback I've ever seen," a beaten veteran Kansas City player said in the loser's locker room. "He is the man, more than Hornung, more than Taylor, more than anyone else they have over there, who puts points on the scoreboard, that makes winning a habit at Green Bay."

JOE NAMATH—
SUPER BOWL III

In the history of pro football, there has never been a player who has received more publicity than Joe Namath. From the time he first put on his white football shoes, he was always the player about whom others talked. A University of Alabama star, he was lucky enough to play for one of the greatest coaches in history, Paul "Bear" Bryant, who called Joe "the greatest athlete I have ever had." Bryant made that statement for a very good reason. Joe started 30 games at quarterback for Bryant in three years and won 27 of them. Among the games he played in his college career, Joe started in the 1963 and 1965 Orange Bowls. He won the game's Most Valuable Player Award in the 1965 game.

That was the year he signed a $427,000 contract with the New York Jets of the American Football League. Joe's contract changed the face of sports. Suddenly players could earn very big salaries.

The story of Joe Namath—his trip from Beaver Falls High School in Pennsylvania, to the University of Alabama, to the New York Jets and football immortality—took fifteen years. During that time,

Joe played some great football, some good football, and too often, no football. Much of his career was marred by injuries.

An important part of the Joe Namath story took place off the field. Joe liked to go out and have a good time. He never tried to hide that fact. When he played for the New York Jets in the 1960s and 1970s, there were many parties in his Manhattan penthouse apartment. His clothes were flashy. For a while, he wore a long, glamorous fur coat that the media was constantly focusing on. He was one of the first players to wear long hair, a practice coaches of the era didn't like. As a matter of fact, the only thing coaches did like about Joe was the way he played the game.

Joe liked to tease people. He liked to laugh and sometimes liked to play the wise guy. More than once, while someone was trying to have a serious conversation with him, Joe would clown around. If the person was from the press, he might take it the wrong way and write a bad story about him. Certainly Joe's image wasn't as good as it might have been if he had been a modest person.

As much as Joe partied, and as much as he fooled around, only serious injury interfered with the way he played football. He would become angry if someone suggested that his football play was suffering from his off-the-field activities. He hated to read that he would play better if he partied less, but it was written often.

"It's not easy for me to be serious for any length of time," Joe once said. "I prefer a good laugh to a good lecture. But I'm serious about football, and I'm serious about using my talent to the fullest.

I stay in shape. I've never been overweight. I've never been too tired to play my best game of football.''

Joe loved football, of that there can be no doubt. Once, when given the choice of making a lot of money or playing football, Joe chose football. Then he was a partner in a New York restaurant. Unfortunately for Joe, the commissioner of the National Football League, Pete Rozelle, learned that gamblers were hanging out in Joe's restaurant. Commissioner Rozelle didn't want any NFL players in regular contact with that kind of people, even in the off-season. Since he knew he couldn't order the gamblers to stay away from Namath's restaurant, he told Joe to sell the place and stay away from there. At first, Joe refused to sell, feeling that the commissioner had overstepped his authority. Before the next season started, however, Joe sold his part of the restaurant. The thought of a season without football was worse than losing a chance to make money.

Joe Namath practiced hard and played hard. There was a time at Jet practices when the offensive and defensive linemen made a deal to protect each other. They agreed that, on plays when the offensive linemen were supposed to hit the defensive men at the knees, one of the guards would tip off the defense by shouting out, ''Fire, protection.'' The defensive linemen would then slow down their charges, and there wouldn't be any rough contact. The players practiced this way throughout the afternoon.

One night, Joe had a talk with a few of the linemen. He said he wasn't getting the kind of practice work he needed because the defensive linemen weren't charging the way they would in a game. "I don't think you can give 100 percent in a game," he said, "if you don't give 100 percent in practice." The linemen agreed, and the practice of tipping-off was stopped.

As good as Joe Namath was, no one will ever know how good he might have been. Namath played an entire career on two bad knees. Because he was so good, so valuable, and so wide open at quarterback, opponents would often go out of their way to crack into his knees. Every season, his knees got worse. In his final year in football, playing for the Los Angeles Rams, Joe could no longer run with his teammates. Instead, after every practice he would swim a distance equal to what his teammates ran in order to protect and strengthen his knees.

Joe played with pain. He had several operations on his knees. Before he could play in any football game, he would slip both his knees into braces, then wrap enough tape around them to satisfy a mummy. This was necessary in order to keep his knees steady. Despite this handicap, he was still one of the best quarterbacks of his time.

"It was quite a feat for Joe to go out there with those old-man's knees," said teammate Sam DeLuca, a starting offensive guard when Joe played with the Jets. "It's tough enough to play football when all the parts of your body are working properly. When you can go at only half speed, you have to be thinking: 'How will I do it? Will I get hurt because I can't go all out?' It has to affect you. Not once in all the years Joe played did I hear him complain about pain, or use the knees as an excuse when he had a bad day."

Football-happy Joe Namath.

Joe Namath grew up in Beaver Falls, Pennsylvania, a small town where most of the men worked in the nearby steel mills. He was born on May 31, 1942, the fourth son of Rose and John Namath. Throughout his boyhood, his family lived in a narrow, white frame house with the bathroom in the basement.

Joe's family was not rich. His mother made a little extra money on the side by working as a maid. Still, Joe had a happy childhood. "I'm glad I grew up in Beaver Falls," he said early in his pro football career. "It was a great place to grow up, with good people, real people, and a river and woods and athletic fields, and rock fights and junkyards—everything a kid could want."

Joe began throwing a football when he was six years old. His older brother, Bob, who was the quarterback for a junior high-school team, taught him how to hold the ball, how to throw it quickly, and how to make it spiral perfectly. Joe was never allowed to wind up. Instead, brother Bob made him throw from his ear.

Because of those early lessons, Joe was almost always the quarterback when he and his friends played football. He was still a quarterback when he went to Beaver Falls High School, but because of his tremendous athletic talent, the coach also made him play defensive back. Joe was equally good at both positions. He was both an excellent basketball and baseball player. Baseball scouts were sure he would be a major leaguer. When Joe graduated from high school, he was swamped with college football scholarship offers. He also had an offer from the Baltimore Orioles. They said they would give him a good amount of bonus money if he would sign with them.

It was a very hard choice for Joe to make. If he went into professional baseball, he would be able to bring money into a family that could use it immediately. If he went to college, he would have to wait four years before he cashed in on his athletic talent. But Joe's family had never had anyone graduate from college, and his mother urged him to be the first. Joe turned down the offer from Baltimore and accepted a scholarship to Alabama.

The University of Alabama's campus is in Tuscaloosa, Alabama—a long way from Beaver Falls. The distance quickly made Joe homesick, and he had trouble concentrating on his studies and making friends. He considered leaving school and taking the baseball offer. But a former major-league pitcher, Bubba Church, who had pitched for the Phillies, the Reds, and the Cubs in the early 1950s, convinced Joe that he would be better off staying in school.

Joe stayed, and things did improve. He was a quarterback seemingly designed by a computer. He dropped back to pass as quickly as anyone ever had and got rid of the ball at once. He was almost impossible to sack. He threw with perfect form, using the overhand motion his brother Bob had taught him. There wasn't a pass that he couldn't handle with great skill. If the ball had to be drilled hard to get to a receiver, he could do that. But he also had the touch to throw feathery balls that would drift over the hands of defenders into the extended fingers of his receiver.

When Joe arrived at Alabama he was a marvelous runner, the type of quarterback who could drive defenses crazy by earning extra throwing time with his scrambling. Then one day, he wrecked his knee. He was just standing on the field when his knee caved in. Eventually, Joe had numerous operations on both knees. The many surgeries robbed him of the mobility that could have possibly made him the greatest quarterback of all time.

A number of great players left the college ranks to become professionals after the 1964 season. Among them were Gale Sayers, Dick Butkus and Joe Namath. The war between the leagues was at its peak then, so Joe was picked by both the St. Louis Cardinals of the NFL and the AFL's New York Jets. The Jets had a new owner, a man named David "Sonny" Werblin. Werblin had been a prominent show-business agent and believed in the "star system." He thought people wanted to see stars in football the way they liked to see stars in the movies. He thought Joe Namath could be a star. He also knew the American Football League needed a gimmick to attract attention away from the NFL. Clearly, the older league was winning the war against the AFL.

Werblin gave Joe a $400,000-plus contract, which immediately made Namath the hottest topic in the sports world. The Jets' owner wanted publicity. He wanted people talking about the AFL. That was one of the major reasons he gave Joe that unheard-of amount of money. After Namath was given the money, people were constantly arguing if Joe, or any other player, was worth $400,000.

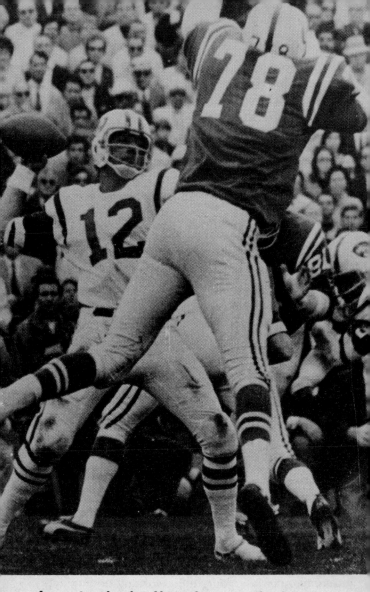

A spectacular Joe Namath passes the Jets to their first Super Bowl victory.

Werblin's plan was successful. The National Broadcasting Company, which had been considering giving up their rights to telecast AFL games, immediately signed the league to another contract. The New York Giants of the NFL, who had been the darlings of New York sports fans for more than a decade, were pushed into the background. All anyone wanted to talk about was Joe Namath. As the season grew closer, the talk about him and the Jets and the American Football League increased.

The group of people who were most skeptical of Joe were his soon-to-be teammates. Most veteran players weren't very happy about the money Joe would be getting when they looked at their own paychecks. In those days, players didn't have agents representing them, so no one was around to explain that Namath's salary would eventually raise their salaries as well. They thought that, as proven players, they should be making more than this untried rookie.

When training camp opened, the veterans badgered Joe quite a bit. They teased him, made wisecracks about his money, and hit him extra hard in scrimmages even though it is part of pro football's code not to hit your quarterback in practice. They were demanding he prove he was capable of making the team.

There were times Joe couldn't take part in regular team drills because he was still recovering from a serious knee operation. While other Jets would run laps around the field, Joe would stand and wait for them to finish. That didn't go well with some veterans. "What's the matter, Rookie?" they would yell. "Are you too good to run? Is your money belt weighing you down?"

The resentment continued all through the pre-season camp. Finally, at a team meeting, Joe spoke up. "Some of you guys don't like me," he said, "but I don't care because I don't like you either. I mean, I don't know you very well so I can't like you or dislike you, but from the way you act, I don't like you. All I'm asking is that you don't judge me for the money I got or the publicity that comes my way. Judge me by what I do on the football field."

That made sense to the players. They decided to ease up on him and give him the chance to prove himself as a football player. He did just that. Passing well, calling plays as if he were a veteran rather than a rookie, he was voted the 1965 AFL Rookie Of The Year.

By the time the 1968 season started, Joe's teammates were certain he was something special. They backed up their thoughts by voting him the team's offensive captain. Now as they ran in the July heat and Joe stood, unable to run because of his knees, he felt good. He glowed in the respect his teammates gave him. When he heard a player run by shouting at him, "What's the matter, Namath? Are you too good to run?" a big grin appeared on his face.

As a matter of fact, his teammate was right. Joe *was* too good to run. It was very important to the Jets' chances of winning that he stay healthy, for Joe Namath was about to turn the football world around for the second time in five years.

In the National Football League, the Baltimore Colts had ended the Green Bay Packers' dynasty, winning the older league's 1968 title. They prepared to enter Super Bowl III as heavy favorites. Their opponents would be Joe Namath and the Jets. The New York team had made it to the Super Bowl after defeating the defending AFL champion Oakland Raiders, in a thrilling game. Now they would try to be the first AFL team to win a Super Bowl.

In both previous Super Bowl games, the Green Bay Packers had won easily. Most of the American public thought the Colts would win easily. It would be a crucial game for the young league. Another Colt victory would lessen the already low opinion most fans had of the AFL. An overwhelming defeat could even mean that the merger agreement the two leagues had signed might be put in danger. After all, if the NFL could whip the AFL at will, why should the NFL play them? And why would fans pay to see them play?

In the two weeks between the championships and the Super Bowl, football people try to squeeze as much publicity out of the game as possible. With one sentence, Joe Namath got more publicity for the Super Bowl than any game has had before or since.

The brash, young quarterback, only 25 years old, met Colt defensive lineman Lou Michaels in a bar the week before the game was to be played. They argued back and forth, each one telling the other how good his team was, and how they would wipe the field up with the opponent come Sunday. Soon the two were yelling, and the possibility of a fight loomed. They were separated, but not before Namath told the Colt that, not only would his underdog Jets do well against the Colts on Sunday, but there was no doubt in his mind that they would win. In fact, he guaranteed it. The press was quick to pick the quote up and turn it into page-one news all over the country.

Come Sunday, half the country wanted to see the young quarterback get his ears pinned back. The other half wanted the underdog team to slay the giant. Everyone knew that, to beat the Colts, the Jets needed an almost perfect game from Namath. They got it.

Protected from the Colts' strong pass rush, which had dominated NFL opponents all year, Namath completed 17 of 28 passes for 206 yards. Eight of his passes were caught by split end George Sauer. But it wasn't only the passing that marked this as a day Joe Namath played a special game. He ran his team as if he were the conductor of a great orchestra. Every time he wanted something out of an instrument, he made the correct gesture. And every instrument he called on performed magnificently. By gaining 206 yards through the air and another 142 on the ground, the Jets attack was so complete that the Colts never knew what to look for.

The moment that best illustrates this game happened late in the first half. New York was leading 7-0. The Jet defense had intercepted two passes thrown by Baltimore quarterback Earl Morrall. One ball was stolen on the Jet two-yard line. Besides that, Lou Michaels had missed two field-goal chances. Suddenly, the Colts became frantic.

With less than a minute to go in the first half, Don Shula's Colts tried a trick play. They were second and nine at the New York 41 when Morrall handed off to halfback Tom Matte for an apparent sweep of right end. That same play had gained 58 yards in the previous series. While flanker Jimmy Orr drifted downfield alone, completely overlooked by the Jet deep defenders, Matte stopped short and threw a long, lateral pass back to Morrall. Standing alone in a corner of the field near the goal line, Orr jumped up and down, waving his arms, hoping Morrall would see him. Earl Morrall never did see Jimmy Orr. Instead, the short pass Morrall threw was intercepted and so were the Colt hopes.

In the second half, Joe Namath, using mainly his running attack, grinded the Colt defense into the ground. Behind fullback Matt Snell, the Jets controlled the ball and the game. Joe's guarantee had held. On that day, and throughout the rest of his pro career, Joe Namath proved that he was one of football's great quarterbacks.

OTIS TAYLOR—
SUPER BOWL IV

The man was built like a football dream. He was 6-foot-3 and 220 pounds—and oh, did those defensive backs hate to see him lined up across from them. His nickname was "Slug," because he always moved so slowly, so sluggishly, until the play started. But once the ball was hiked, he moved like the wind. He had a sprinter's speed, a tight end's strength, and hands that held onto almost everything they touched. In short, Otis Taylor may have been the most perfectly assembled pass receiver in football history.

Opposition coaches feared him. When they drew up their defensive game plans, they made sure that Otis would be covered closely. Despite all the attention, Otis was still able to catch over 400 passes in his career.

In the mid-1960s, it was normal fare for various American Football League coaches to argue who was a better pass receiver—Kansas City's Otis Taylor or San Diego's Lance Alworth. Most were inclined to agree with the Boston Patriot assistant coach who said, "Toss a coin." But by the 1970s, the ratings had changed. Taylor and Alworth were no longer mentioned in the same comparison. There were few who disputed that Otis was the best all-around receiver in football. He was capable of grabbing the long bomb, but he also consistently caught the short pass. At the beginning of every season, the Kansas City coaching staff would mark down 40 receptions next to Otis' name as the amount they expected him to catch. Usually, he would exceed that number. It was also a yearly tradition for Otis to be among the league leaders in points scored, with all of his touchdowns coming on pass receptions. But what set Otis Taylor apart from other wide receivers was his blocking. He was a devastating blocker in a position where most prefer not to get their uniform dirty.

"If you can make a block and open a path for a touchdown for someone else," Otis said, "that can be as rewarding as catching the ball and running 80 yards for a touchdown."

At 6-foot-3 and 220 pounds, Otis certainly had the size to be a good blocker. But to be a good blocker, a man must have a strong desire and a lot of heart. Many a man with great size has been a poor blocker because he has a peanut-sized heart. Otis' heart was as big as Texas, the state he was from.

Otis Taylor was also a great jumper—a skill he developed as the center for the Prarie View A&M college basketball team. Quarterbacks love to throw to a man who could jump like Otis. Often, he would turn an overthrown pass into a completion. He would transform sure interceptions into long gains. And if he couldn't catch the ball himself, he would bat it away so the defensive man couldn't snare it.

Taylor was the type of receiver who was routinely expected to make incredible plays. During a game in 1967, Kansas City quarterback Lenny Dawson threw a pass to Otis that was five yards too short. As the Jet cornerback and safety moved to the ball, Otis ran between them, jumped as high as he could and caught the ball with one hand. That one-handed catch was no accident. In practice, Otis would regularly practice "impossible" catches. He would ask the quarterbacks to throw the ball to him poorly so he would have to do something special to make the catch. For a time, he would try catching the ball only with his left hand. Then he would shift to right-handed catches. He would ask for catches for which he would have to dive. He would even attempt to catch the ball with his hands behind his back. He knew that a ball could come to a receiver in many different ways during a game, and he wanted to practice catching them all. Otis Taylor tried to prepare for everything.

In a game against the Washington Redskins in 1971, Otis ran a long pattern, then cut across the end zone. At the right moment, Dawson threw a spiral pass. Pat Fischer, a smart cornerback, saw that the taller Taylor was about to catch the ball so, in desperation, he grabbed Otis, pinning his left arm to his side. With his free hand, Otis reached up and plucked the ball out of the air for a one-handed touchdown catch.

Some fans, and even some coaches, were fooled by Otis Taylor's slow-moving ways between plays early in his career. They thought he was lazy, but actually he was saving energy. It was an old trick, one the great

Jim Brown, the NFL's all-time leading rusher, used when he played. Like Brown, Otis would get up very slowly and almost wobble back to his huddle after a play. Come the next play, he would gain 20 yards. He would seem to have trouble making it back to the huddle again, but then he would gain another 20 yards.

"Otis had a deceptive way about him," said Lenny Dawson. "He'd seem to be gliding along, and then suddenly he would take off. But what I liked about throwing to him was not only did he have good hands and fast feet, but he was smart. He saw the whole field. He'd come off the field and draw plays in the dirt. We scored more than one touchdown on plays Otis drew."

Once in a game against the San Diego Chargers, Otis loped through what the Chiefs called "backside patterns", the patterns a receiver ran when he was not the primary target. Each time Otis ran a backside pattern, he noticed that the defensive back, Speedy Duncan, would cover him a little more loosely. It seemed to Otis that Duncan wasn't paying enough attention to him. During a time-out, Otis drew a play for Dawson that he thought would work. Dawson agreed to try it.

On the snap of the ball, Otis looked like he was just loafing through the play, running out another backside pattern. Suddenly, he took off. He dashed right by a startled Duncan, caught the pass, and raced half the field before he was caught. By using his mind as well as his body, Otis had put the Chiefs into scoring position.

Otis Taylor.

Otis Taylor was born August 11, 1942, in Houston, Texas, the son of a school custodian. Otis' heart was always in sports, but football was not Otis' first love—baseball was. Then he swung over to basketball, admiring the way Elgin Baylor danced his way through the game. Taylor, a high-school forward, dreamed of being Baylor. "I saw Elgin Baylor while I was in high school and couldn't believe the man," Otis said. "I tried to do the things he did. I wasn't a great shooter, but playing basketball helped me as a football player. It made me quicker and more agile."

In his younger days, Otis' position in football was quarterback. He was blessed with a powerful throwing arm and was able to whip a ball 70 yards. Then, the time came to choose a college. He decided to stay in his home state and go to Prairie View A&M.

Otis Taylor was still a quarterback when he entered Prairie View A&M. In his sophomore season, an assistant coach noticed him catching passes on the sideline. The coach saw that Otis would grab the ball with one big hand. From then on, Otis was a pass catcher, and Jim Kearney, who would later be Otis' teammate on the Chiefs, became the team's quarterback.

"Jim and I did some fantastic things together at Prairie View," Otis remembered. "He would just tell me to go out and run, and he'd get the ball out there 50, 60, 70 yards."

In 1964, Otis' senior year in college, the American and National Football Leagues were in the middle of a war for football talent. Scouts offered decent salaries and good-sized bonuses to players to come with their league. These scouts used all sorts of tricks to lure players into signing with them. Although Otis came from a small school, both the NFL's Dallas Cowboys and the AFL's Kansas City Chiefs were after him. One day, a man who worked for the Cowboys called and invited Otis to a party in Dallas. Otis went to a Dallas hotel where he found a number of other good college players who had also been invited to the party.

Meanwhile, the Chiefs were trying to find Otis because they also wanted his name on a contract. A Kansas City scout, Lloyd Wells, who had once worked for the NFL, came to Dallas to locate Taylor. He couldn't. He called the Chiefs' offices in Kansas City to tell them that, even though he had followed through on every tip he had been given, the Cowboys had successfully hidden Otis. He said he thought he might as well come home. The Chief higher-ups told him to stay in Dallas and look some more. They wanted him to sign Otis.

Finally, Wells found a girl who knew where Otis was, but she wouldn't tell the scout. Wells phoned up Otis' mother and told her the whole story. Mrs. Taylor hung up the phone, called the girl, and in no uncertain terms told her to tell Wells where her son was. The girl told Wells that Otis was at a motel in a Dallas suburb. Quickly, Wells rode to the motel.

Otis was enjoying another party at the motel. A Prairie View teammate, a huge defensive tackle named Seth Cartwright, had also been invited. During the party, a Dallas scout made the mistake of telling Otis that Cartwright was only a decoy to keep Otis there. The Cowboys, the scout said, weren't interested in Cartwright as a player.

Otis was angry. His teammate was being used. A few minutes later, a Cowboy official told Otis that a newspaperman wanted to see him. Otis went to the door where the "newspaperman" turned out to be Lloyd Wells. Quickly, Wells explained that he had to say he was a newspaperman or the Dallas people would never have let them speak. He told Otis he was being held prisoner, but that he would help him bust out if he accepted the Chiefs' contract offer. If he signed to play for the Chiefs, he would get a car, a bonus of $10,000, and a $14,000 salary—a big offer in those days. The Cowboys had made a similar offer, but after the party, Otis had decided to hold off making a decision. Now he made a decision to sign with Kansas City.

It was almost midnight when the party ended. The Cowboys had rented rooms at the motel for the players so that they wouldn't be contacted by AFL teams. Wells left the motel, then drove his car to a small road within sight of Otis' room. Then, as in a James Bond movie, he sat in his car and waited.

At three in the morning, two figures scurried out of a motel window, ran around the pool, and headed for his car. Wells started his car engine and flung open the door as Otis and Cartwright jumped in. Wells gunned the motor and swiftly drove away. A huge smile crossed his face—he had pulled off a cloak-and-dagger operation and had come away with Otis Taylor.

Otis Taylor was a tremendous asset to the Kansas City team. Those long Dawson-to-Taylor passes put a new zip into the Chiefs' offense. "We used to travel by bus," head coach Hank Stram used to say, speaking about the Chiefs' offense in the franchise's early years. "With Otis, we go by jet."

Stram wasn't the only member of the Chiefs' family who felt strongly about Taylor's contributions. "The biggest factor we had going for us when we won the championship was Otis," said Fred Arbanas, the Chiefs' All-Pro tight end. "He gave us the long-ball threat, and he blocked. Otis didn't mind sticking his nose in there."

The Kansas City Chiefs leaned on Otis Taylor to make the big play for more than a decade. But probably the biggest play Otis made in his career was against the Minnesota Vikings in Super Bowl IV.

That Super Bowl must be remembered against the backdrop of the times. The previous year, the New York Jets had defeated the Baltimore Colts for the AFL's first victory. Most experts, however, had written the result off as a fluke. In Super Bowl IV, the experts predicted, the Chiefs would be beaten easily. The AFL would be put back into their place. Thus, once more, an AFL team was put into the unenviable position of representing the league's right to exist. A Kansas City loss would reflect badly on the entire American Football League just as the merger of the two leagues was going into effect.

The Chiefs took the early lead and were dominating the game. At halftime, the score was 16-0, but early in the third quarter, the Vikings mounted a drive. Minnesota halfback Dave Osborn took the ball in for a score. The Vikings were alive.

But the threat did not last very long. All day, a key play in the Chiefs' attack had been the end around, a play as old as the game of football. Lenny Dawson had used it by dropping back as if he were going to pass, then putting the ball behind his back so that speedy wide receiver Frank Pitts could take the ball from him and run with it. The first time Dawson called for the "52 go reverse", the Chiefs name for the play, Pitts swept right end for 19 yards. The second time, late in the second quarter Pitts gained 11 more yards. In the third quarter, Dawson used it once more. Again Pitts circled deep behind Dawson, took the ball, and tried to circle the end. This time, the Vikings were ready. But Otis Taylor laid a crunching block on the great Carl Eller, and Frank Pitts was still able to scamper for seven yards and a crucial first down.

"Otis got some great crackback blocks on Eller today," Pitts said after the game. "His blocks made the play work all three times." With the ball on the Viking 46, Dawson dropped back to pass and fired a short one out to the right flat. Otis caught the ball. Just as he gathered it in, Viking cornerback Earsell Mackbee hit him full force around his thigh, then bounced off. With Mackbee out of the way, Otis set sail for the end zone. Running along the sideline, Taylor's next obstacle was safetyman Karl Kassulke, who cut across the field and attempted to block Otis out of bounds. Otis gave him an inside fake, then broke free and scored. The game was over. The Chiefs had won and had upheld the reputation of the American Football League.

The big win also added to the reputation of Otis Taylor. Not only would people become aware of how great a football player he was, but his national press exposure let people know what his philosophy was.

"I am not an athlete for the money or the fans or the Super Bowl," he said. "I am an athlete for my own heart."

ROGER STAUBACH—
SUPER BOWL VI

In 1963, Roger Thomas Staubach became the fourth junior in college football history to win the Heisman Trophy, the award given annually to the nation's best player. An outfielder and pitcher on the baseball team, numerous major-league scouts were quick to say that Staubach would earn at least a $40,000 bonus if he went with their sport. Scouts from both professional sports knew that here was an athlete of enormous physical gifts and amazing emotional stability—a dream prospect.

In November, 1963, the Kansas City Chiefs of the American Football League acted on their dream and drafted Roger even though he was only a junior. After graduating from Cincinnati's Purcell High School, Roger attended New Mexico Military Institute for one year. Under the drafting rules of the American Football League, a player could be picked the year he was supposed to graduate, even if he was a year late in getting his diploma. Using a 16th round choice, the Chiefs drafted Roger as a "future."

The National Football League had already done away with its future rule. Thus they didn't draft Roger till a year later, when he completed his education at the Naval Academy. In the 1964 draft, Dallas picked Roger on the 10th round. That a player of Roger's ability and prominence was still around so late was due to the fact that, before Roger could play pro football, he would have to spend four years in military service. Dallas drafted him because they felt they had nothing to lose. When he played his last collegiate game, pro scouts shook their heads sadly.

Their sadness was understandable. Though several great athletes who had played at service academies (Army, Navy, Air Force Academy) had served in the armed forces of the United States, then went into pro sports, none had ever recaptured their form. Great players like Army's Glenn Davis and Navy's Joe Bellino, both speedy halfbacks, were shadows of themselves after they left the military. If Staubach were to ever try the pros, most figured, the odds were stacked against him ever being a dominant player.

The odds against the Cowboys getting even a serviceable player, let alone a star, would have multiplied greatly if it had been known that part of Staubach's military duty would be in Vietnam at the height of the conflict. Only Roger and Pittsburgh's Rocky Bleier had made it from the Vietnam war zone back to the comparative safety of the National Football League's playing fields.

But that's getting ahead of our story. Staubach first gained attention as the most unpredictable passer/scrambler in college football. At Navy, he would stand behind the center, a slim figure in gold, staring at the enemy over the backs of his crouching linemen. "Haaaay, set! Hup-ah-hup-ahhup-ah-hup, hup, hup..." The ball came back, and the spectators held their breath. *"What will Staubach do this time?"* they wondered. First Roger was rolling right, fading back as if he were going to pass. Then he was slithering away from one tackler, straight-arming another. Downfield, three receivers zigged, zagged, looked back, then zigged again as they tried to stay in position for a Staubach pass. Behind the line of scrimmage, Roger wasn't ready to pass yet. He moved back and forth, he was trapped, he dodged out of the trap and was loose again, he raised his arm to pass, then lowered it. In a burst of swivel-hipped speed, he suddenly dashed forward, past the line of scrimmage. He ran for five yards, for ten yards, for a first down and more.

Another play: the same thing. But this time, he stopped on a dime to throw a perfect spiral 17 yards downfield. Touchdown!

A movie script? Not at all. It was just Roger Staubach playing college football. Unrestricted by the professional football notion of what a quarterback should and shouldn't do, he gambled and scrambled and was always a sight to see. Just ask the 37,000 screaming fans who saw him against Southern Methodist University in 1963 if they ever saw a better or more exciting college football player.

Roger Staubach prepares to pass.

The night they invaded the Cotton Bowl in Dallas to play SMU, Navy's Middies were rated the number-one team in the country. The SMU team was all fired up. If they could beat the number-one team in front of the home folks, it would make their season, no matter where they finished in the Southwestern Conference standings. They played with tremendous verve and fire, so much so that, early in the first quarter, a vicious, but clean, blindside tackle sent Roger Staubach to the bench with a stretched nerve in his left shoulder. Five minutes later, as if nothing had happened, Roger was ramming himself through the center of the SMU line for a touchdown.

But the SMU Mustangs were hot. They scored twice before half time. Still, Roger managed to keep Navy ahead. He set up one touchdown by rolling to his right for long yardage. He set up another by rolling to his left, also for long yardage. At the half, 31 points were on the scoreboard: Navy 18, SMU 13.

Early in the second half, a jarring tackle sent Staubach sprawling once more. His left shoulder was in pain again, but since it wasn't his throwing side, he decided to act like nothing was the matter. He stepped back and calmly pitched a touchdown strike to raise the Navy lead to 25-13. All Navy needed to win now was a stout defense. They didn't get it. In two plays, the Mustangs scored again. Minutes later, SMU got another touchdown and jumped into a 26-25 lead.

It was Roger's turn. Circling right end, he picked up 11 yards, getting stopped by a herd of Mustangs who trampled him near the sidelines. Slowly, the tacklers unpiled. A gasp went up from the stands. Roger lay stunned on the ground.

If ever a man played like Superman, it was Roger on that day. After smelling salts revived him, he was ready for more action. He moved the Middies to the Mustang two-yard line. A field goal put Navy ahead, 28-26. With two minutes and 53 seconds left, a bruised, battered, exhausted Staubach dropped onto the bench. He hoped the defense would run out the clock. Not today. SMU traveled 70 yards in four plays for a touchdown. Score: SMU 32, Navy 28.

It seemed too much to hope that Roger could rally the Middies again. Time was against him. With less than two minutes left on the clock, Navy was more than 60 yards from the SMU end zone. Roger began to work his magic again. He scampered around right end for 16 yards. He passed for 14 more. Another pass for 12 yards. He ran the ball up the middle himself for 15 yards. With two seconds to go and the ball on the three, he fired his last pass to an open halfback in the end zone. But the halfback just dropped the ball. Despite Staubach's most magnificent performance, Navy was beaten for the first time in the 1963 season as Roger walked off the field weeping.

The SMU game lead opposition coaches to rave about Staubach. "Just say he's terrific," an eastern coach said. "He's head and shoulders above all the other quarterbacks," another eastern coach agreed. "He's an unbelievable passer, a beautiful scrambler and has great vision. But more than anything, it's his running that makes him nearly indefensible. Plus he's an inspirational leader."

The recipient of this praise, Roger Staubach, was born on February 5, 1942, the only son of Mr. and Mrs. Robert Staubach. Early on, it became clear that Roger was the original Wheaties ad—neat, well-mannered, studious, and explosive on the football field. He had the whole city talking about him when he was a senior at Cincinnati's Roman Catholic Purcell High School. There, he crossed up arch rival Elder High's defense and carried the ball 60 yards on a bootleg play for the winning touchdown. College scholarship offers poured in. According to Roger's mother, legendary Ohio State coach Woody Hayes "must have spent a fortune in telephone calls trying to recruit Roger." But the one college Roger yearned to go to—Notre Dame—gave him the polite brush-off. After that, when Navy people told him it was time for him to think about what he could do for his country, Roger signed to go to Annapolis. "I decided I wanted to do something else in life besides play football," he said.

Getting an appointment to the Naval Academy was easy; getting in proved more difficult. Roger flunked the English section of the entrance exam. The Naval Academy foundation—a private organization, the Navy was quick to point out—paid his way to New Mexico Military Institute for a year of English cramming. He passed the entrance test on the second try.

From that day until he joined the Cowboys, Staubach lived under the rules of military life—as a cadet at the military institute for a year, as a midshipman at the Naval Academy for four years, and as a supply officer in the Navy for four more years. Coming to the Cowboys, and to the discipline that Coach Tom Landry preached, was a continuation of the life he had known for nearly a decade.

On July 5, 1969, Roger's active tour of duty ended, and he quickly shifted uniforms: from Navy blue to Cowboy blue and silver. On that same day, Don Meredith, who had been the Cowboy quarterback since the franchise was started in 1960, announced his retirement. With Meredith gone, back-up Craig Morton moved into the number-one quarterback slot, with Staubach as his back-up. Without having done a thing, Roger Staubach moved closer to becoming a first-string quarterback in the NFL.

It takes a while for a quarterback to learn the pro game—any quarterback—but especially one who had been away from organized football for four years. It wasn't until midway in the 1971 season that Staubach got his chance to start. Early in the season, Coach Tom Landry had alternated Morton and Staubach as the starters. By the seventh game, the Cowboys record was only 4-3. Three of the victories and none of the defeats came when Staubach started. Landry benched Morton, started Staubach on a regular basis, and the Cowboys became unbeatable. They won their last seven regular season games, then defeated Minnesota and San Francisco for the National Conference title, and went on to beat Miami in the Super Bowl.

In Super Bowl X, Staubach's Cowboys lost to the Pittsburgh Steelers, 21-17.

"Morton never had a chance," said Bob St. John, a reporter who covered the Cowboys for a Dallas newspaper. "He was trying to lead a normal life. He'd finish the day tired and want a beer. Staubach would still be out there running laps and throwing passes. I used to watch Staubach and think, 'I'm glad he's not after my job.'"

Roger was tough. Early in his career, he was intercepted four times in an exhibition game against Baltimore. The Colts won easily. Even though he had problems passing, he still ran for more than 100 yards. Roger sweated off 15 pounds that hot August night, but that was a drop in the bucket compared to what Baltimore's huge defensive lineman, Bubba Smith, lost. "I hate Staubach," Smith said after the game. "I never ran so much in my life chasing anyone. I never want to play against that guy again."

As Roger learned more about NFL quarterbacking techniques, he scrambled less out of desperation and more out of design. He ran for first downs, but not because he couldn't find his receivers. "One criticism of Roger was that he had a slow delivery," said Ermal Allen, then Tom Landry's special assistant. "When he came to camp in 1972, he had one of the fastest deliveries in the game. Like with everything else, Roger had understood what his weakness was and worked on it so much that it had become a strength."

As Roger grew more experienced, he seemed to have that special talent to be able to win games that looked like lost causes. In an early season game in 1972, Roger tried to run over a linebacker and wound up with a separated shoulder. With Morton at quarterback, the Cowboys made the play-offs. In a play-off game against the San Francisco 49ers, the Cowboys trailed by 15 after three quarters. At that point, Landry rushed a rusty Staubach into the line-up. With two minutes left in the game, Dallas still trailed by 12. Then Roger took the team to a quick touchdown. The Cowboys recovered an onside kick, and Roger struck again—another touchdown and a Cowboy victory. Staubach did the same thing in the 1975 play-offs when he threw a game-winning pass that Drew Pearson caught despite being harassed by defenders.

The image the American public has of Roger Staubach is that he is a man who is almost perfect and always nice. For the most part, that image is right. He is a religious man and makes no effort to hide that fact. He has been called a "square." When he was voted the Most Valuable Player in the Super Bowl game against Miami, he told the magazine that presents a new sports car to the award winner that he didn't want the sleek Dodge Charger. His family needs were more along the line of a station wagon. The magazine gave him a station wagon.

Roger was named Sports Father of the Year and Dallas Chairman of the Hemophilia March of Life Brigade. He was also a member of the Salvation Army. He was the clean-cut, patriotic athlete, the All-American boy who had grown into an outstanding citizen.

That didn't mean Roger wouldn't do a stunt to get a laugh. From time to time, he pulled some dillies. Once, he showed up at the Cowboy's executive offices in search of team president, Tex Schramm. When Roger came in, Schramm was in the middle of a long-distance telephone call. While Roger fidgeted in his chair, Schramm rocked in his. He made no effort to shorten the call, turning his back to his desk and looking out the big picture window. Soon Staubach got up and found a janitor who led him out to a narrow, unrailed ledge eleven stories above the parking lot. Roger made his point by leaping into Schramm's view. The startled Cowboy president gasped, "Oh, my God!" as he almost overturned his chair.

It was time for Super Bowl VI, as Dallas prepared to play Miami. Ever since the first Super Bowl, the Cowboys had been close to winning everything, but always a little short. The previous year, they had lost super Bowl V, 16-13, when Baltimore kicked a late field goal. They had also lost NFC championship games in the last seconds to Green Bay twice in the 1960s. Frustration was the team's middle name. When Super Bowl VI began and Roger missed a few open receivers, Cowboy fans expected the worst again. Maybe it was true, they thought, that our team can't win the big games. But Roger Staubach was a leader, the kind of man who got better when the situation was difficult. Coach Landry, who called all the offensive plays, instructed Roger to go to a running game. The result was that Duane Thomas, Walt Garrison, Calvin Hill and Roger combined for 252 yards rushing. With Roger in control, the Cowboys played without mistakes while the game was still in doubt.

Staubach led the Cowboys to victory in Super Bowl XII as Dallas beat Denver, 27-10.

If there was a point that seemed to move the Cowboys close to victory, it came with 75 seconds left in the first half. The Cowboys had the ball on the Miami seven-yard line, first down. Wide receiver Lance Alworth went down to the corner of the end zone, where he was closely guarded. Staubach drilled a pass to Alworth, who somehow grabbed the ball through a windmill of arms, and quickly stepped into the end zone. The pass was so perfectly thrown that the Dolphin defender had no chance to bat the ball away. The touchdown gave Dallas a 10-0 lead, and they never looked back. The Cowboys won, 24-3. The frustration plaguing the Dallas Cowboys had finally melted, thanks to the skill and leadership of the great Roger Staubach.

LARRY CSONKA— SUPER BOWL VII

There are rumors that Larry Csonka was not born, but assembled at a truck plant in Detroit. At a playing weight of 237 pounds mounted on a 6-foot-2-inch frame, Csonka's body looked like a tractor trailer used in long-distance hauling. Actually, Csonka's hauling was more of the short-distance variety. He averaged slightly more than four yards per lifetime carry—good, but not spectacular. As a matter of fact, Larry was rarely spectacular. He would just grind an opponent into the dust. Every week, he made thrust after thrust into the defensive lines, and by game's end, the defensive line was giving ground, and Larry Csonka still driving ahead. Third and one, third and two, fourth and one—those situations were Larry-time. Larry would never leap into the air, but rather put his head down and power his way to countless first downs. Miami never would have won two Super Bowls without the consistency of Larry Csonka.

Larry loved his job. He loved playing fullback, and he did the job well. He ran, he caught passes, and he blocked. He especially loved the feeling of hitting and being hit. He loved the sight of the collisions. He loved the sound of them. "The noise is great," he said once.

"At the snap of the ball, the first noise you hear is defensive ends slapping their taped hands against the helmets of our offensive tackles. At the same time, there's the clack of shoulder pads hitting all along the lines and the grunting of linemen as they collide. It's really neat.

"Going through the middle with the ball, you hear all that noise and you see the guys being blocked. They're going down with this wild look in their eyes. They're clawing and scratching, reaching out at you. You have this tremendous feeling of being protected by your offensive line. You see these guys fighting to bust you up, but they're walled off and that's a great feeling. If you had the time, you'd chuckle. 'Ha, ha, ha, you can't catch me.'

"Running a sweep, I'm just trying to get away," Larry continued. "But running up the middle I'm challenging them. I prefer that, because up the middle I know they're going to be waiting."

Larry Csonka was a bulldozer, a battering ram, someone who kept his cutbacks to a minimum. Time and again, you can see on films of Larry's runs that he took the direct route even if there was a man or three in his way.

Larry's directness, both on and off the field, were important factors that went into making the Miami Dolphins the best team in football. He and his close friend, Jim Kiick, formed the best running pair in the league in the early 1970s. Neither of them was fast, but Kiick was a bit fancier. In describing their different running styles, Jim said, "I like to run where there are holes; Larry likes to run where there are people."

Kiick, like Csonka, was an excellent blocker. He was also an excellent pass catcher, as sure-handed as any receiver in football on third down plays. Both men played when they were hurting. Neither blew assignments, and both rarely fumbled. One year, between the two of them, they carried the ball 448 times and fumbled only once. The fumble was Kiick's.

"Kiick and Csonka," a rival coach once lamented. "You can't spell them, and you can't stop them."

Because of their friendship, they picked up their nicknames, Butch Cassidy and the Sundance Kid, after the title of a popular movie of the time. A poster with Larry and Jim in western costumes sold very well all over the country. The two were very popular. Once, the president of a Washington D.C. woman's organization walked into the Redskins' office wanting to buy 5,000 tickets. She said her group wanted to see an exhibition game. When asked which game in particular, she answered, "I want to see Butch Cassidy and the Sundance Kid."

Lawrence Richard Csonka was born on January 1, 1946, in the small town of Stow, Ohio. He was raised on an 18-acre farm there. His father, Joseph, worked at the Goodyear Tire plant in Akron, Ohio. It was from his father that Larry got his size and strength. Larry remembers that, when he was a kid, his father could be very tough on him. Mr. Csonka would have Larry hoe beans "until I wanted to hit him with the hoe." Larry and his brother slept together in a rough board attic where it was so cold, "I could watch my breath go the length of the room. I had a runny nose the first ten years of my life.

"I hated the farm until I was old enough to know better," Larry continued. "Now I know how rewarding it was—growing things, having animals."

Farm life was also rewarding to Larry's body. The hard work made him strong, big, and powerful. "He was so big for his age," Mildred Csonka, Larry's mother, said, "that people thought he was much older. He had to take his birth certificate along to prove his age when he signed up for Little League baseball. He liked playing baseball, but when he was 11 or 12, he refused to go back. One of the coaches begged him, but he wouldn't. I think it was partly because he'd grown so much bigger than the others that he was embarrassed. But that was also about the time he discovered football."

Larry weighed 150 pounds when he was 12. By the time he was a high school junior, he had tried every position on a football field, including quarterback. "There was something about throwing the ball," he said. "I didn't want to turn it loose."

Larry was a very good football player in high school, good enough at the fullback position to win a scholarship to Syracuse University. Even though he went there as a fullback, in his sophomore year, Coach Ben Schwartzwalder converted him to linebacker. "It was the biggest mistake I ever made," Coach Schwartzwalder later admitted. "The smartest move I ever made was converting him back to fullback when he was a junior."

Larry was an eager learner. He wanted to be as good as he could as quickly as he could. He was willing to try anything he thought would improve either his mind or body. Once a Syracuse tackle told him he could strengthen his forearms by banging them into hard objects. Larry was envious of the size and strength of the tackle's forearms. That summer, coach Schwartzwalder got a call from Joseph Csonka, Larry's father, who asked the coach to get Larry out of his house. He was knocking down the walls, according to Mr. Csonka, strengthening his forearms.

"Actually," Larry said, "it was only one wall, and it was coming down anyway."

Back at fullback, Larry broke every Syracuse rushing record. There had been great runners at Syracuse before Larry, people like Jim Brown, Ernie Davis, Jim Nance, and Floyd Little. "I'm not really in their class," Larry modestly said, "I just carried the ball more." When Larry broke the last of Little's records, they stopped the game to give Larry the ball as a souvenir. Larry flipped it to the sidelines. "I didn't know what they were doing," he said. "I thought the ball was no good and they were changing it."

After college, Larry was drafted by and signed with the Miami Dolphins of the American Football League. Before reporting to the Dolphins' training camp, he went to the College All-Star camp near Chicago. In those days, the NFL champion would play a charity game against the best college players entering the pro ranks. It was quite an honor to be chosen to play for the All-Stars. It was also a hardship. An all-star would practice with this makeshift team for three weeks.

In 1974, Miami beat Minnesota, 24-7, as Csonka rambled for two touchdowns.

Meanwhile his new team would be playing the other rookies who reported to their camp on time. All-star rookies often had bad first seasons because of that.

It was at the 1968 all-star camp that Larry Csonka first met Jim Kiick. Csonka had been Miami's first-round draft choice, Kiick, the Dolphins' fifth pick. Csonka, who had gotten a $100,000 bonus to sign with Miami, went on to be the game's Most Valuable Player.

Kiick never got in. Norm Van Brocklin, the All-Star's coach that year, said Jim was too fat, too slow and had a bad attitude. "I did have a bad attitude," Jim said, "when I realized he could say all that without seeing me play." Larry Csonka obviously saw things in Kiick that Van Brocklin missed. When the two players arrived in the Dolphins' traing camp after the All-Star game, Larry told Miami writers that Kiick was a guy that they had better get to know. He was a terrific player who was going to be around for a long time.

Because they came to the Dolphins' camp together, Larry and Jim were thrown together as roommates. For the rest of their careers, they were roommates by choice. Kiick was awed by Larry.

"He was huge," Jim remembers. "I was embarrassed to be around him. He was taller and stronger than me. I measured my thighs and was happy that they were 28 inches. His were bigger. The guys on the team kidded him every time he ran downfield on a pass pattern: 'Lineman down field!'

"We were nothing alike, but we hit it off. Larry likes to fish. I hate the outdoors. But I could enjoy it with him. I like to play basketball or shoot pool. He doesn't give a damn but he'll come watch."

Four years after Larry and Jim joined the Dolphins, Miami had become a very good team. In 1971, Larry gained over 1,000 yards (1,051) for the first time in his career. In the AFC championship play-offs that year, the Dolphins and Kansas City played a Christmas Day game that lasted into the sixth period, the Dolphins finally breaking the tie with a field goal. Three weeks later, the Dolphins appeared in their first Super Bowl.

On January 16, 1972, they played the Dallas Cowboys in Super Bowl VI. The Cowboys were looking for revenge, having lost to the Baltimore Colts the previous year. There were hints early in the game that this would not be the Dolphins' day. Taking a hand-off from quarterback Bob Griese, Larry charged into the line, was hit by a Dallas linebacker, and fumbled. It was the first time Larry had fumbled all year, after 248 carries. It was an omen. Miami lost 24-3. They vowed to be back. They kept their vow, returning the next two years.

During the 1972 season, it seemed like everybody connected with the Dolphins was working a little harder. The entire organization was determined to go back to the Super Bowl to win. They won all 14 regular-season games, then won the two play-off games that put them into Super Bowl VII. This time, their opponents would be the Washington Redskins, coached by tricky, old George Allen. The Redskins had defeated the defending champion Cowboys in the NFC title contest, 26-3, and believed they were a team of destiny.

Dolphin coach Don Shula went into the Super Bowl with a problem. Early in the season, his first-string quarterback, Bob Griese, had been injured. He was replaced at quarterback by Earl Morrall, who had taken the Dolphins this far. Now Griese was healthy, and clearly he was the better quarterback. Yet the Dolphins had won with Morrall, and Shula was reluctant to break up a winning combination. Taking all factors into consideration, Shula decided to go with his best, Griese. He knew Morrall was an old pro, who knew he had been hired to be Griese's back-up. With Griese ready to play again, he knew Morrall would understand.

The Dolphin strengths were Griese's passing to Paul Warfield, the running and catching of Jim Kiick, the running of Larry Csonka, and the play of their defense, nicknamed "the no-name" defense. Despite an impressive record during the season, the unit didn't get any publicity. After the Super Bowl game, however, men like defensive tackle Manny Fernandez and defensive end Bill Stanfill were no longer overlooked.

The Dolphins played a smart Super Bowl game. They used their strengths well. Griese used Csonka especially well. He gained 112 yards that day—more than any running back on either team. Larry's running allowed the Dolphins to maintain ball control. There was little doubt that the Dolphins would win. The final score was 14-7. In winning, the Miami Dolphins became the first team in NFL history to finish a season undefeated.

The most memorable moment of the game came with little more than two minutes left. The Dolphins were winning 14-0 and driving toward another score. All day long, they had been able to do pretty much what they wanted. The fourth quarter was no different.

The final Dolphin drive stalled inside the Redskin 30. Coach Shula decided to go for a field goal to ice the game. Place-kicker Garo Yepremian attempted a 42-yard kick, but the Redskins got to the ball and blocked it. The ball bounced directly back to Garo, who made the mistake of not trying to fall on it, but rather picking it up. Attempting to throw the first pass of his career, Garo let the ball slip off his fingertips into the hands of Washington defensive back Mike Bass who ran untouched into the end zone for seven points. A few minutes later, after one final defensive stand, the Dolphins were Super Bowl champs, 14-7.

The Yepremian comedy bit and Csonka's running are the memories of Super Bowl VII.

The following year, the Dolphins won the Super Bowl again, Larry rushing for 145 yards this time. In Super Bowl VIII, Csonka was the Most Valuable Player. In the two most important games of his pro career, he gained more than 100 yards both times. Larry Csonka, the hard-hitting, bulldozing fullback, proved himself to be a valuable player, indeed.

LYNN SWANN—
SUPER BOWL X

On a hot August afternoon on a Little League diamond outside of San Francisco, 11-year-old Lynn Swann was playing left field. He looked funny in his baggy-pants baseball uniform. It was so big on him. Even his cap was too big.

It was the last inning of the game, and Lynn's team, the Senators, were in the lead. Then somebody on the other team cracked a sure home run to left field. Everybody said, "It's gone. That's it. The game's over." But all of a sudden, Lynn, baggy pants and all, ran back to the outfield fence. He reached up, made an impossible leap, and snagged the ball that had already cleared the fence on the tip of his glove. It was no home run—just a very long out. The Senators won. If the Washington Senators had gotten plays like Lynn's from some of their outfielders, they never would have moved to Minnesota.

No one who saw the catch could believe it. How could someone so small and skinny and wearing such a ridiculous-looking uniform make a catch that saved the game? But Lynn did. Though he's changed his sport and now catches footballs instead of baseballs, Lynn makes the same kind of catch he made on that baseball diamond nearly twenty years ago every week in front of millions of people.

Lynn Swann not only catches the ball as well as or better that any other wide receiver in football, but he also does it with much more flair and style than any of his colleagues. Every time Lynn goes up for a ball, you can see his 14 years of ballet training. You can also see the hours he spent in the sand pits, practicing long jumping. When he was in high school, Lynn was the California state long-jump champion with a best distance of 25′, 4½″. There are those who say he might have gone to the Olympics in that event if he had only continued to work at it.

But he didn't. Football became Lynn's main sport. He had always played ball in the shadow of one of his older brothers, Calvin. When it came time to go to high school, Lynn won a scholarship to a private, Catholic high school, Serra. Calvin, a year older, went to the local public school, San Mateo High. Calvin had always been the better athlete, but in high school Lynn caught up. Both brothers did very well in football, so well in fact that the 1968 game between Serra and San Mateo was billed as a grudge match between the Swann brothers. Indeed, the arguments at home became so loud that Lynn moved in with his coach until after the game. Both brothers played spectacular football that day, each catching two touchdown passes. The final score was Serra 57, San Mateo 33.

Lynn's athletic reputation began to grow. He decided to go to the University of Southern California because it was one of the best football schools in the country. Throughout his career at USC, he ran, blocked, and caught passes. According to his head coach, John McKay, he was excellent in all those areas. He was also used as a punt returner. Lynn did so well in all his roles, that he was named to the 1971 All-American team. In the 1973 Rose Bowl, he gave a preview of what to expect when he caught six passes for 108 yards and one touchdown. The only regret Coach McKay had after Lynn's final game at USC was that he wouldn't be a Trojan anymore.

He would be playing for the Pittsburg Steelers, another winning outfit. Lynn was the Steelers' first-round draft choice. The year Lynn came out of college, the Steelers had a great draft. Besides Lynn, they picked wide receiver John Stallworth, linebacker Jack Lambert, and strong safety Donnie Shell. At the begining of training camp that year, the NFL veterans were on strike. Lynn felt compelled to be something of a squad leader until they came back. He filled that role very well.

By Swann's second season, the Steelers were bound for their second straight Super Bowl triumph, this time with Lynn as a starting wide receiver. Lynn replaced Ron Shanklin, a top-notch pass catcher, who would have started for most other teams in the league.

As a rookie, Lynn's pass-catching grace was much more impressive than his statistics. Given little

Leaping Lynn Swann does it again!

opportunity from the line of scrimmage, he caught only 11 passes for two touchdowns. He was, however, turned loose as a punt returner. That year, he led the NFL in punt-return yardage, taking one punt all the way back for a touchdown.

That second season, 1975, Lynn startled most every cornerback he played against. Besides catching 49 passes and a league-leading 11 touchdowns, he caught balls he had no business reaching. Once Willie Alexander, a fine cornerback for the Houston Oilers, who went up against Swann many times, talked about Pittsburgh's number 88. "He isn't the swiftest runner in the league. He doesn't have Isaac Curtis' speed. But he always gets to the ball."

Lynn Curtis Swann was born on March 7, 1952 at Alcoa, Tennessee. The rumors that he could gracefully jump out of his crib at three days of age are untrue. That he was an excellent young athlete is very true. Lynn grew up in the San Francisco suburb of Foster City, California. Like most California youngsters who want to play ball, Lynn had tremendous access to sports. He played often, and he played well. He loved to play and soon found he had all the ingredients necessary for a career in pro sports.

By his mother's insistence, however, Lynn had to look at more things in life than sports. While his father worked the night shift at the nearby airport, Lynn's mother would give him Bible lessons. She took him to restaurants so he would learn the proper way to dine. In order to help him experience some of the finer aspects of art, she had him take tap dance and ballet classes. Those lessons are so apparent whenever you see a slow-motion replay of one of his remarkable catches. Lynn was a regular visitor to museums, art galleries, the theatre, and ballet recitals. Because of his mother's insistence that he be exposed to many things, these days Lynn is more than just a football player. He writes poetry, collects fine wines, and works as a television news reporter in the off-season.

Throughout his pro career, many of Lynn Swann's opponents have tried to stop him. They've tried all kinds of schemes, yet have failed even to slow Lynn down. Since Lynn weighs only 172 pounds, many defenders have thought the way to stop him is to intimidate him. Many have tried, none have succeeded.

One who tried hard was former Oakland Raider defensive back, George Atkinson. Two weeks before Super Bowl X, Lynn was carried off the field after being hit in the head by Atkinson. In the first game of the following season, Atkinson hit him in the head again, using his taped forearm like a club. Again he knocked Lynn out, and again Lynn had to go to a hospital. This time, Lynn protested and threatened to retire. "The game is tough enough within the rules," he said.

A lot of people reacted to what Lynn said. They said he was a sissy, a crybaby, a tattletale, a California big shot who had appeared on television too often. They pointed out there wasn't even a penalty called on Atkinson's hit. All-time great receiver Lance Alworth said that, for his part, he always considered cheap shots to the head a compliment. "I don't want a compliment that could end my career," Lynn replied sensibly.

Touchdown, Swann!

After looking at the films of the play, the National Football League agreed with Lynn and fined Atkinson for what he did. The films showed there should have been a penalty on the play. Lynn was on the side of the field away from the ball. Swann was completely out of the play, and the ball was thrown to another receiver.

Because Lynn spoke out, the NFL put in a rule that made it illegal for a defender to hit a receiver more than once on any play. Soon after, another rule was added that says a defensive man can't bump a receiver more than five yards past the line of scrimmage. The league began to look thoroughly at game films and fine people they found playing illegally.

"I think if you do a study of well-known cheap-shot artists," Lynn said soon after the rules were changed, "you'll find a number of them are either sitting on the bench or out of the league." Though Lynn didn't say it, George Atkinson left the league shortly after the rules were changed.

Though Lynn's size is a detriment on the football field, off the field, Lynn finds it a big help. Often people will come up to him and say, "You know, you look just like Lynn Swann." Lynn answers, "Yes, but I'm not big enough to be him."

Fame has brought other things to Lynn. It has brought him the chance to be the only football player to be a ballet trustee. In 1980, he was named a trustee of the Pittsburgh Ballet Theatre. "He was a likely candidate because of his dance background," a Pittsburgh Ballet Theatre spokesman said. "We asked him, and he accepted without hesitation."

Before the 1976 Super Bowl, Cliff Harris reopened the question about Swann's courage. He predicted that he and other Dallas deep defenders would intimidate Lynn. He thought he could scare him out of the game. Many fans and opponents thought Harris made sense. It didn't make sense to Swann's teammate, Rocky Bleier, who had been wounded in Vietnam and knew more about courage than most. He said: "I think some defensive backs say, 'This guy got hit once and cried about it. I'll rap him a good shot, and he'll quit.' Lynn attracts that kind of attitude. But he takes it."

Lynn also gives it. If he's made a routine touchdown catch, he'll casually toss the ball over his shoulder. But if he's made the play over a back who's been bothering him, then he'll give the ball the classic spike—a sort of "How's that, Turkey?"

The smart thinking before Super Bowl X was that the Steelers would win the game only if fullback Franco Harris trampled the Cowboy defense. If he didn't have one of his better days, most experts saw the Cowboys coming out on top. They were wrong. Dallas held Harris fairly well in check, but they couldn't do a thing with Lynn Swann, Terry Bradshaw, and a defense that could take apart an attacking tank battalion.

Mainly it was Swann who kept his team in the game when it seemed to be slipping toward the Cowboys. With the Steelers down 7-0 in the first quarter, Lynn soared above Cowboy defender Mark Washington and grabbed a 32-yard Bradshaw pass for a first down. The great sideline catch helped keep a Steeler drive going and, a few minutes later, the score was tied.

Then in the fourth quarter, Lynn made the biggest catch of the day, a 64-yard touchdown pass from Bradshaw. When the referee's arm went up after the point after touchdown, the Steelers had a safe 21-10 lead.

Lynn's two plays have to be dwelt upon. The first one took place in front of the Steeler bench. Steeler coach Chuck Noll was standing only a few feet away from where the catch was made. Noll is not a man given to easy praise. If praise comes out of his mouth, it has been earned.

Noll said: "Lynn Swann has a sixth sense to go for the football and catch it. To catch that pass and stay in bounds, he had to make an S-curve of his body. It was miraculous."

The last catch had Super Bowl trophy written all over it. There was so much to the play, so much that could have happened, and so much that did. It ended with Lynn catching a 70-yard rocket from Bradshaw. Lynn jumped and took it on the Dallas five-yard line, then glided into the end zone for the touchdown. Meanwhile, a barely conscious Terry Bradshaw was lying on the field, the victim of a hit by Cliff Harris, who arrived an instant too late on a safety blitz.

The play began with the Steelers leading 15-10 and just over three minutes left in the game. It was third down and four at the Steeler 36. Dallas wanted the ball back badly. If they could get it, Roger Staubach would have plenty of time to manufacture the winning touchdown.

Swann makes another amazing touchdown catch, this time against the Rams in Super Bowl XIV.

Bradshaw tried the long pass when the rest of the world expected him to go for the first down. His call shocked his critics, who enjoyed calling him a "dumb" quarterback. The play outfoxed the Dallas defense, and then Lynn Swann outjumped them.

What made Lynn's performance all the more remarkable were the circumstances. It was not known until right before the game if he would be able to play at all. He was still suffering after-effects from the concussion he received in the AFC title game two weeks before. Lynn felt fine, thought he could play, but Chuck Noll didn't tell him he was starting until just before the opening kick off. That's when he decided he couldn't win without Lynn.

Noll was right. After the game, Lynn was voted the Most Valuable Player Award. Clearly nothing Cliff Harris said or did had affected Lynn in the least. In fact, it made him a better player that day. Lynn Swann had truly risen to the occasion.

FRED BILETNIKOFF— SUPER BOWL XI

Fred Biletnikoff truly loved to play football. If the game of football had been a woman, he probably would have married it. In a way, he *was* married to it. Biletnikoff played 14 years in first the AFL, then the NFL, sat out a year, then went to Canada in order to catch square-out passes one more time.

To understand why Fred wished to push the clock back, you only have to look at his statistics. He caught 589 balls playing for the Oakland Raiders. Though he was never fast, Biletnikoff had extraordinary moves and a quick burst of speed toward the ball once it was in the air. He also had sticky fingers—if his hands touched a ball, he rarely dropped it.

Fred wasn't an immediate starter with the Raiders. He wasn't the fast, eye-catching type of receiver, the kind of pass catcher who gets an automatic opportunity. Coaches dream of blue darts, guys who catch 80-yard passes, then stroll into the end zone. Slower receivers, "move men," are usually in a coach's plans, but never in his dreams.

To a coach, a slower man means his offense will have to work hard for whatever it gets. That's the bad news. The good news is that a move receiver like Fred Biletnikoff will hold onto every ball thrown his way, run the right pattern every time, and be in the right place at the right time so the patterns that depend on timing will work.

Fred did not get an opportunity to show how good he could be until halfway through his rookie season. He came to the Raiders in 1965 out of Florida State. In training camp that summer, he led the team in worrying. Every time he saw a Raider coach shake his head, he was sure that he would be cut. When he heard one say he thought Fred was too slow to make it in pro football, he felt even lower than usual. The more he worried, the worse he played. Even in practice, his chances to show what he could do began to diminish. When he got into scrimmages or games, he dropped balls. "What's the matter with you?" a friend asked him one day after practice. "You caught all those passes in college. You were an All-American. Why can't you catch them in the pros?"

The 6-foot-one, 195-pound Biletnikoff frowned. "In college, it was easy to run patterns," he said. "You ran out and cut left or right. The defensive backs were afraid you would run deep for the long pass, so they let you have the short ones. The pros don't give you anything. Besides, it's hard learning to be at the exact place at the precise time. I make one false step, and I'm either too late or too early. Everything—all the patterns, all the signals—they seem so difficult. I never learn anything fast. When I go out to catch a pass, I'm thinking too much about the pattern. I'm not concentrating on the ball, and I drop it. I know they're going to cut me.''

Fred was wrong. The Raider organization is run by Al Davis, who many people consider the smartest man in football. There was no way someone as smart as Davis would make a mistake about someone as talented and dedicated as Fred Biletnikoff. Maybe Davis didn't know how good Fred would become, but he did know that Fred would be good. When he retired from the NFL after the 1978 season, Fred was the fourth-ranking pass catcher in history. Only Washington's Charley Taylor (649), Don Maynard (633), who played with three teams, and the Baltimore Colts' Raymond Berry (631) had caught more than Fred.

Part of what made Fred great was his attitude. Even after he proved he was a good pass receiver, he was still worried. In practice, he would yell loudly at himself if he dropped a pass. The day before a game, he would sit moodily in front of a television and hardly speak. The morning of a game, as soon as he woke up, he would complain. Sometimes he would complain about the noise in the hotel. Other times, he would complain about the air conditioning, about the hardness of the mattress he had just slept on, or the poor television reception in the room. ''Two groans and a grumble,'' his roommate, Tom Keating would say. ''That was Fred's idea of good morning.''

Then the game began, and the emotional Biletnikoff would make the opposition pay for his bad frame of mind. Once he was playing against the New York Jets, and one of their cornerbacks,

Johnny Sample, began to pester him. He insulted Fred, threatened him, did everything he could to get Fred to break his concentration. "You'll drop it, you'll drop it, you stink," he would shout whenever Fred ran a pass pattern.

Fred caught a pass. He caught another pass. Then another. And another. Soon Sample was playing the game in silence. "I like to play against guys like that," Fred said afterwards. "If you catch a few on them, they suddenly stop talking. They know and you know that you've whipped them."

Fred liked to dress slowly after games. "He's still worried," Tom Keating once said to a newspaperman. "It will take him eight hours to calm down."

Fred himself said on more than one occasion that he thought he worried too much. "But look," he said. "I didn't have the great gifts when I came into the pros. I couldn't run with the speed of a sprinter like Bob Hayes. I didn't have the natural moves of a man like Raymond Berry. Since I was a kid I wanted to be a professional football player, and I was afraid I didn't have enough God-given talent to make it. So I worried."

Raider coaches agreed with Fred when he said he didn't have a great deal of natural talent. But they meant it as a compliment. "The thing that was impressive about Fred," said long-time Raider head coach John Madden, "is that he was a man-made receiver. Some guys are just gifted, almost animal in their moves. Not Fred. He's had to work for everything he's got.

"Fred caught the ball at his ankles on the one-yard line."

"His greatest ability was, once he touched a ball, he held onto it. Most pro receivers have good hands for catching a ball, but Fred went beyond that. He caught balls others would just write off. He had tremendous concentration, and when the ball was in the air, he wouldn't think about anything except catching that ball."

Most people remember the great game Fred Biletnikoff had in Super Bowl XI. In 1968, he played in a game that was of extreme importance to the Raiders and played as well as he did in the 1977 Super Bowl game. If the Raiders won the game, they would be champions of the AFL's Western Division. That meant they would earn the right to play for the AFL title. Fred caught seven passes for 180 yards and three touchdowns in that game. Even more startling than his statistics is the man he did it against, Emmitt Thomas, one of the best cornerbacks ever. But Fred had to pay a price for doing such bad things to Thomas. Early in the fourth quarter, Fred was sent to the sidelines for injury repairs.

"I don't bother anybody out there, I just go about my business," Fred said after the game. "When you're out there running your patterns, you just run. Thomas caught me under my helmet with his fist. I got kind of scared. I wasn't knocked out, I was just real dizzy. I didn't know where I was either, which is what scared me."

The Raiders beat the Chiefs 41-6 that day and won the Western Division title, but they lost the AFL championship the following week to Joe Namath and the Jets.

Fred Biletnikoff grew up in Erie, Pennsylvania. From the time he was first able to play ball, he dreamed of catching long touchdown passes in front of huge crowds. He would walk down the wind-whipped streets of Erie and actually see himself running under a long bomb, then gently placing the ball on the ground after the touchdown.

Fred always wanted to be a pass receiver. No other position on the field interested him. "I wouldn't know where else I'd play if not outside receiver," he said. "I've always liked catching passes. Split end or flanker are the only positions I could play."

Fred was lucky. Erie High, where he went to school, used a pro-set offense and passed all the time. They scored touchdowns on long passes with great regularity. Unfortunately, they allowed touchdowns on long passes with even greater regularity. "We didn't win a lot," Fred once said, "but we sure were exciting."

In Fred's last year at Erie High, a Florida State coach watched him catch passes on film. That year FSU was switching to a pro-type offense. They had already recruited a quarterback who could throw, Steve Tensi, and they thought that Fred had the hands necessary to hold onto his line-drive passes. Fred hadn't received many scholarship offers. Too much daydreaming about long passes made for less than good grades. So when the offer from Florida State came in, Fred quickly accepted.

Biletnikoff gave Florida State two fine years at wide receiver, and he ended his college career with a great year. In his senior year, Fred wound up fourth in pass catching in the nation. He and Tensi made a great passing team. Together, they put Florida State on the football map. Tensi, a 6-foot-5 stringbean quarterback with a powerful throwing arm, would rifle passes into the hands of the tricky Biletnikoff. In their senior year, they both made a number of All-American teams. In the 1965 Gator Bowl, Fred caught four touchdown passes from Tensi, a wonderful way for both of them to end their collegiate football careers. As their teammates ran off the field celebrating the 36-19 victory over Oklahoma, Fred signed a pro football contract with the Oakland Raiders under the goal posts.

Almost immediately after reporting to the Raiders' camp that summer, Fred wished he had signed with the Detroit Lions of the NFL who had also drafted him. He had signed on with the AFL Raiders because he thought that Detroit had so many good, young receivers he would never get a chance. Now, with the Raiders, his nightmare seemed to be coming true. The Oakland team had him competing for a job against Bo Roberson, a fast, young receiver who had been a world-class sprinter and long jumper in college. Roberson was one of the reasons Fred never got his jersey dirty in the first six games the Raiders played in Fred's rookie year.

Fred nervously waited. There was little else he could do. The Raiders seemed committed to Roberson, for the time being at least. The Al Davis offense called for many long passes every game. But soon it became evident that, even though the Raiders were throwing many long passes every game, most were falling incomplete. With all his speed, Roberson was not making anything happen. Finally accepting the fact that he was a track athlete who looked good in a football uniform until the ball was in the air, the Raiders traded Roberson. They brought Fred off the bench. In the second half of that season, he caught 48 passes.

The next year, Fred ran into a series of injuries. The most serious were to a knee and to an eye. After surgery on the knee, Fred favored the repaired leg. Each time he ran, he wondered if it would collapse under him. Before the start of the 1967 season, he told the Raiders' other wide receiver, Warren Wells, "I'm afraid to plant the knee. I'm thinking so much about the knee that I'm dropping passes."

The Raiders were getting ready to play an exhibition match with their cross-bay rivals, the San Francisco 49ers. Before the game, Fred found out that, following the game, eight players would be cut. "They're going to cut me," the second-year receiver told anyone who would listen. "Nobody told me, but I can feel it in the atmosphere. You get that feeling when you're a regular who they're playing in garbage time, and when the coaches are hardly talking to you." His voice tightened. "I'm too nervous to talk about it."

When the game began, Fred tried to forget about being cut. Early in the game, he was supposed to cut into the middle of the field, then get past defensive back Kermit Alexander. But Alexander was playing him inside, so Fred faked that way, then veered to the outside, toward the sideline, hoping that old pro quarterback George Blanda would see what he was doing and adjust. Blanda did. He threw a pass to Fred near the sideline, and it became a 41-yard touchdown. The next morning, the Raiders cut eight players. Fred was not one of them.

Fred Biletnikoff went on to become one of the most consistent pass receivers in football history. When the game was on the line, he was even better than usual. Raider quarterbacks George Blanda, Daryle Lamonica, and Kenny Stabler all knew to look in number 25's direction if they needed to complete a pass late in a crucial game. For some reason, Fred Biletnikoff, like so many great athletes, seemed to get better in tough situations.

There was no situation better suited for Fred to show off his talents than Super Bowl XI. The Raiders had just missed making their second Super Bowl appearance on a number of occasions. Something always seemed to block their way. Now they were finally in again. Eighty million football fans would be waching. For Fred, it was that boyhood dream come true. He would snare passes while everybody in America watched.

The Raiders' opponent was the Minnesota Vikings. They were led by quarterback Fran Tarkenton. The Vikings had already played in three Super Bowls, all losses. They wanted a victory in the worst way.

The Raider plan was clear from the beginning. They would run behind the left side of their line, where guard Gene Upshaw and tackle Art Shell played. Upshaw and Shell were two of the best

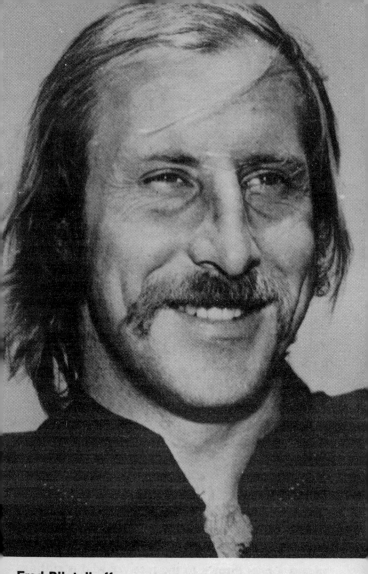

Fred Biletnikoff.

players ever at their positions. They were 550 pounds of quickness, muscle, and experience. In the first half, the Raiders used 20 running plays. Seventeen went to the left side. Journeyman halfback Clarence Davis, running mostly to the left, gained 137 yards during the game. But it was the passes thrown by Kenny Stabler to Fred Biletnikoff that sealed the Vikings fate that day.

Prior to the game, the Raiders thought that Biletnikoff would be open because they expected the Vikings to concentrate on stopping Cliff Branch, the Raiders' wide receiver on the other side. Branch had once been a world-class sprinter. Oakland loaded up its game plan with passes to Biletnikoff. But the Raiders' pregame thinking was wrong. Fred had to fight his way through traffic to get anywhere on the field. The Vikings sought to bottle him up. They had watched films and decided that it would be difficult for Stabler to go away from his favorite receiver. But they couldn't bottle Fred up forever. Midway through the second quarter, with the Raiders leading 3-0, Stabler hit Fred, who made a nifty catch and ran the ball down to the Minnesota one-yard line. On the next play, the Raiders scored.

Before the pass to Biletnikoff, the following conversation took place in the Oakland huddle. Stabler said to Fred, who had a history of speechlessness at these moments, "Do you want anything?"

Biletnikoff gave a one-word answer; "Post." Post means a pass thrown to the receiver who is cutting toward the goal posts.

The play went off. Fred caught the ball at his ankles on the one-yard line. In describing it later, Stabler said, ''Fred never likes to say anything. I have to beat if out of him.'' Fred nodded, then laughed. ''It was the first time I said anything in the huddle all year.''

It wasn't the last pass he caught all day, however. Less than four minutes later, Biletnikoff made a sliding 17-yard catch that took the ball back to the Minnesota one-yard line. Again the Raiders scored on the next play, padding their lead to 16-0. The Vikings never got close, and the Raiders won Super Bowl XI 32-14. Even though Fred didn't score a touchdown, he did catch four passes, two that led directly to scores. Because of that, he was voted the game's Most Valuable Player. A magazine rewarded him with a car for his performance. When last seen, Fred was worrying about what he would do with it.

TOM LANDRY—
SUPER BOWL XII

There are those who say Tom Landry has done more for the hat industry in America than anyone since Alice in Wonderland's Mad Hatter. The people who make that judgment are not in professional football. Pro football people will tell you Tom Landry has done more for defense than anyone. Landry's thoughts, methods, and ways of playing defense have been copied by most NFL teams. Even though his ideas on defense are now more than 20 years old, they still hold up. Tom Landry has always been a man ahead of his time.

That Tom Landry should be a designer of new ways to play football may seem strange to those who see him only on television. After all, he seems so conservative, so settled, that one would never get the impression that he searches for new answers. The man the public sees could be called "The Great Stone Face." Along the sideline he never laughs, rarely smiles, moves sparingly, hat firmly in place. When his Dallas Cowboys are on offense, Coach Landry calls all the plays. Concentration is his middle name. Emotion seems foreign to him.

Defeat is another foreign object. For 15 consecutive seasons, from 1966 to 1980, his teams have had winning records. Despite not having won a game in 1960, his first season as a head coach (which was also the first season for the Cowboys expansion franchise) and, even though the Cowboys didn't have a .500 season until 1965, Landry's coaching record was 199-119-6 at the conclusion of the 1980 season. In addition, Tom is the only coach to lead his team into five Super Bowls, winning two.

Tom is part of an organization. Unlike other legendary head coaches, like Vince Lombardi of the Green Bay Packers and Paul Brown, from whom the Cleveland Browns franchise took its nickname, Tom Landry has not become better known than the team he coaches. Both Lombardi and Brown became stars. When someone thought of the Packers or the Browns, they would think of them first. The fact that both were coach and general managers and in complete charge of their organization partially explains why the men became more famous than the team. They were both rough men who did things in their own manner. They controlled everything and everybody around them.

Tom Landry has been the only head coach the Dallas Cowboys have ever had, yet he doesn't have special authority within the organization. He has but one voice in a many-voiced operation. He has shared power with team president Tex Schramm and vice-president of personnel development Gil Brandt. He has shared newspaper space with team owner Clint Murchison, Jr., who regularly lets the world know that he is one of the richest men in Texas. Tom Landry, on the other hand, is not given to making rash or controversial statements. He is not interested in publicity, though he understands that a football coach is a public figure. Tom Landry is first and foremost a football coach.

Pro football, as it is played today, is a combination of science, speed, and muscle. It is computerized violence, and Tom Landry is undoubtedly the best computer in sports. Computers are not known for their personal warmth or sparkling wit. The people who say that Landry is not a man but a computer, see him so immersed in football films, statistics, and plans that he often misses everything else around him. Once, after working with a new secretary for three months, he picked up his office phone and asked the switchboard operator, "What's my secretary's name?"

Thomas Wade Landry was born to Ray and Ruth Landry on September 11, 1924, in Mission, Texas. His father, a garage owner, also served as Mission's fire chief and the superintendent of the Sunday school where the family worshipped.

At Mission High School, Tom was an "A" student. He was a member of the National Honor Society, president of his class, an all-regional fullback in football, and an outstanding performer in sports generally. He was eagerly accepted as a student at the University of Texas.

In the spring of his freshman year at Texas, Landry joined the United States Army Air Corps. World War II was going on, and most young men were joining up to fight. At age 19, Landry got his wings and became the co-pilot on a B-17 airplane. Stationed in England, Tom flew 30 missions for the Eighth Air Force.

After the war, Tom returned to college and quickly became the University's intramural light heavyweight boxing champion. He also played quarterback and fullback for the Longhorn football team. After his sophomore year, he willingly gave up his quarterback post to Bobby Layne, because it was clear that it would help the team. Layne went on to become one of the great quarterbacks in history.

In his junior year, Tom made the Southwest Conference all-star team as a fullback, and he was honored as team captain when he was a senior. He played on winning Sugar Bowl and Orange Bowl teams in his last two college seasons. Tom graduated from Texas with a degree in business administration. He went on to play pro football, while earning a mechanical engineering degree in the off-season.

In 1949, as a pro football rookie, Tom punted and played defensive back for the New York Yankees of the old All-American Football Conference. The following year, when the AAFC and the NFL merged, Tom moved over to the New York Giants. Tom played cornerback for the Giants from 1950 to 1955. For the last two seasons, he doubled as a player-coach, handling the Giants' defense. In 1954, he was voted onto the NFL's all-pro team.

The late Hall of Fame defensive back, Emlem Tunnell, who played with Landry on the Giants, once said, "You never knew what was going on in Tom's mind. He never said anything. He just always knew what was going on. We didn't have words like 'keying' in those days, but Tom made up his own keys and taught them to the rest of us."

"I was a mechanical engineer by training," Landry explained. "I had to know what was going on. It was my nature. I couldn't be satisfied just trusting my instincts the way Tunnell could. I didn't have the speed or quickness. I had to train myself and everyone around me."

It was that desire to train himself and everyone around him that made Tom into a wonderful coach. "He's the best defensive coach in the business," Jim Lee Howell, then Giants' head coach, said back in the 1950s. No one disputed him then. No one disputes that statement now.

It was while he was with the Giants (he remained with them as an assistant coach through 1959) that Tom changed the thinking of pro football. For years, the Giants had played what was called the "umbrella" defense. That defense set up with six defensive linemen and one linebacker. Tom moved the two defensive ends off the line of scrimmage and made them into linebackers. Suddenly the 6-1 defense became the 4-3. The 4-3 defense is still the basic set-up for the majority of pro football teams. Tom was given complete control of the Giant defense in his last four years in New York, when the Giants regular season record was 33-14-1. They won three division titles and a world championship. Tom's defensive coaching was a cornerstone of those winning New York teams.

In 1960, Tom moved on to become the first head coach of the expansion Dallas Cowboys. That first year, the Cowboys failed to win even one game. They did manage a tie, a come-from-behind affair against his old friends, the Giants. Having to live without

Tom Landry, head coach of the Dallas Cowboys.

topflight talent for a few years, Tom put in an offense with a lot of trick plays. "The trouble with simple football," he said, "is that if every team concentrated on perfecting routine plays, the best athletes are going to win. I reject that as the idea of football. To me, football is a great deal more than just trying to outpersonnel the other team."

The Cowboys, the NFL's first expansion franchise, had to start from ground zero. The team wasn't voted into the league until several weeks after the 1960 college draft had been completed. That first Cowboy team was made up of players the established clubs didn't want. Quarterback Eddie LeBaron was Dallas' only quality veteran player, and the Cowboys were only able to grab him after he announced his retirement. That first year, the Cowboys had 193 players through training camp. "It was like a Greyhound Bus terminal," LeBaron remembered. "During the exhibition games, I was throwing passes to guys I had never seen before and never saw again."

So Landry went to work with rejects, retreads, cripples, and war veterans. He knew he couldn't beat teams straight up. He had to fool them. By 1960, every team had adopted Landry's 4-3 defense. Since it was his baby, he knew its strengths and weaknesses and could create an offense designed to fool the opposition. It included every formation known to man. Motion came from every direction. There were double and triple reverses with passes at the end of the play. The team set up in every way imaginable, trying to get a little bit of an edge on the defense. Even with weak personnel, Landry's offense worked so well that every team in the league began toying with additions to their offense. The defensive "genius" had changed the offense also.

Tinkering with both his offense and defense is a Tom Landry trademark. He always likes to come up with new things that the other teams have to adjust to. While they're adjusting, the Cowboys are winning.

Landry especially loved to tinker when Roger Staubach was his quarterback. Staubach could do so many things well. Once Tom wanted to take advantage of Staubach's great scrambling ability. He also wanted to give his team an edge on the third down and long yardage to go, the obvious passing down. Tom came up with the idea of using the "shotgun" offense, which had been used by the San Francisco 49ers in the early 1960s and was then discarded. In the shotgun, the center snaps the ball to the quarterback, who is standing about six yards behind the line of scrimmage. He is able to see the entire field immediately. "I never understood why a quarterback had to take the ball from center, the way its done in the T-formation, turn and run back ten yards on third and long, when everybody in the stadium knows he's going to pass," Landry said.

Besides the logic in using the shotgun formation in third and long situations, Landry realized that, in Staubach, he had a quarterback who could run. Tom couldn't resist the chance to cross up the opposition in one more place.

Though Tom Landry and Roger Staubach were both serious men dedicated to winning football games, sometimes Staubach tried to lighten up his working relationship with Tom. Once, with the outcome of a game assured, Staubach approached Landry along the sidelines with mischief on his mind. He knew, despite the score, Tom would say the same thing to him for the seven millionth time.

"Just hang onto the ball," Tom said predictably.

"Let me hand the ball off," Staubach pleaded with a straight face. "If I just take the snap and fall it will kill my rushing average." The quarterback waited for a response. A grin. A smile. A snicker. Alas, nothing. Not a crack in the wall.

"Tom didn't do anything," Staubach said later. "I mean, he didn't even look at me."

Don Meredith, once a Cowboy quarterback, could have told Staubach that. Once in a training camp scrimmage, Meredith threw a pass that was intercepted by safety Cornell Green. Meredith yanked off his helmet and chased Green down the field as if he intended to bash him with it. Everybody laughed except Landry. At the team meeting that night Tom said, "Gentlemen, nothing funny ever happens on the football field."

"Everything shuts off in Tom's mind during a game," Gil Brandt, a Cowboy vice-president said. "When Tom's on the sideline, he doesn't even know my name."

It wasn't until 1972, 12 years after he became a head coach, that Tom Landry removed a burden from his back. For years, his critics said his teams couldn't win the "big games." They pointed to the fact that he had never won a Super Bowl, that somehow his team always lost the last game of each season. His critics were factually correct. Twice the Cowboys had lost the National Football League title games to great Green Bay Packer teams in the final seconds. They had lost Super Bowl V the previous year on a last-second field goal. It began to seem to all the world that the Cowboys would never win a Super Bowl until they beat Miami 24-3 in Super Bowl VI.

The Cowboys appeared in Super Bowl X and lost to Pittsburgh 21-17. Two years later, they were back in Super Bowl XII. This time their opponent was Denver, making their first appearance in the season's climactic game. Landry and his staff had assembled a powerful team for that 1978 game. The Cowboys were equally strong on offense and defense. Roger Staubach led the offense. At his beck and call, he had a breakaway runner in Tony Dorsett, four top receivers in wide men Drew Pearson, Butch Johnson, and Golden Richards, and tight end Billy Joe DuPree. The offensive and defensive lines were considerably better than solid. Defensive linemen like Ed "Too Tall' Jones, Randy White, and Harvey Martin made life miserable for the people they played against. Tom Landry had done his job in bringing in this talent-laden team into the play-off tournament and Super Bowl at their playing peak.

Before the game, two points of view dominated.

"We're numer one," says Landry after his Cowboys beat Denver, 27-10, in Super Bowl XII.

Those who favored the Cowboys saw them coming after their former teammate, Craig Morton, now the Bronco quarterback, in waves. Morton's immobility would make him a sitting duck, they figured. Those who liked the Broncos foresaw a low-scoring struggle, with the Denver team forcing a turnover late in the game and winning. The first group was right. The Cowboys won, 27-10.

Super Bowl XII was played in the Louisiana Superdome on the night of January 15, 1978. That night, Harvey Martin and Randy White chased Craig Morton all over the city of New Orleans. The Cowboys, with more talent at every position, were just too good for the Broncos. They had more gifted athletes, a superior quarterback in Roger Staubach, and a very smart coach in Tom Landry.

Late in the game, Harvey Martin sacked a quarterback for the fourth time, causing a fumble on the Denver 29-yard line. As the offense went on the field, Tom told Staubach he wanted him to run "Brown right formation, X opposite shift, toss 38, halfback lead, fullback pass to Y."

The play called for Staubach to hand off to fullback Robert Newhouse, who would pretend to run a sweep to his left. Newhouse would suddenly stop, then hurl a deep pass to Golden Richards who would be racing behind the Bronco secondary. Dallas executed the play perfectly. Newhouse's pass was on the money and Richards cradled the ball as he entered the end zone. Tom Landry had driven the final stake into Denver's heart.

"The thing about Tom Landry," all-pro safety Cliff Harris said after the game, "is when he gives you a play you know it is the best possible play you can have at that moment. He projects security."

One moment in Super Bowl XII symbolized everything about Tom Landry. The Cowboys were penalized five yards for having 12 men on the field. There are people in the NFL who will tell you that the Cowboys *always* have 12 men on the field because Tom Landry helps his players more than any other coach. Supposing that's true, Cowboy opponents are penalized a lot more than five yards every game.

ROD MARTIN—
SUPER BOWL XV

If you want to talk about unlikely Super Bowl heroes, talk about Rod Martin. When people spoke about interceptions by an Oakland Raider in 1980, they would think of Lester Hayes. That cornerback stole 13 passes in the regular season, then five more in the play-offs. Yet it was Rod Martin, not Lester Hayes, who hijacked three of Ron Jaworski's passes in Super Bowl XV.

When people talk about Oakland Raider linebackers, Ted Hendricks is the man they would mention first. After all, he's 6-foot-7, has been in the NFL for 12 years, and has torn up more offenses than a "Mad Stork," his nickname. Yet it was Rod Martin, not Ted Hendricks, who destroyed the opposition's offense by snagging three passes meant for other men.

Rod Martin is the kind of man who humanizes a huge event like the Super Bowl. Heroics have so often come from unexpected people in the baseball World Series. Men like Nippy Jones and Hal Smith surfaced for one big moment, then faded into history. They are part of the lore of baseball. Rod Martin is not nor will he ever be a big star. He is a journeyman player, one who does his job and keeps his mouth shut. He is the first Nippy Jones-type to make a Super Bowl splash. In the long run, his success will do more for the Super Bowl than ten good performances by a proven star.

That Rod Martin ever made it to the Super Bowl is itself quite a story. Both Martin and the team he played for, the Oakland Raiders, didn't figure to make it to the 1981 Super Bowl. Martin had been cut by two teams in 1977. The first team to cut him was Oakland. By all rights, he should have been out of football four years when Super Bowl XV took place.

The Raiders didn't figure to get into Super Bowl XV for a variety of reasons. Before the 1980 season, their management got into a bitter battle with both the NFL hierarchy, led by Commissioner Pete Rozelle, and the city of Oakland. Raider owner Al Davis wanted to move his team to Los Angeles. He thought he could make more money in the larger city. His desire to move seemed to overshadow the football games. The team's legal battle was on the front page of the newspaper daily. Instead of football, team members were asked questions about loyalty to the Bay Area. Suddenly the Raiders, who had been loved for years by the people who live on the eastern side of the San Francisco Bay, were considered traitors. The players took much of the abuse meant for Al Davis because they were visible. The Oakland Coliseum, which had sold out for Raiders games for more than a decade, rarely did so in 1980, even though the Raiders were highly competitive. For the first time since the Coliseum was built in 1966, empty seats were constantly visible.

If the legal battles were not enough, the loss of a long-time quarterback great would have grounded most teams. The Raiders had traded Kenny Stabler to Houston after the 1979 season. In return, they received Dan Pastorini, another veteran quarterback, who Raider management said it wanted to rebuild the team around. Al Davis talked about going back to the long passing attack he had used successfully years before. Pastorini was a reknowned long passer and, at 31, he was four years younger than Stabler. If the Raiders could get lucky, experts thought, Pastorini would be in control of the offense by season's end. Then the team might be a play-off contender. More than likely, however, it would take one full season for Pastorini to become a Raider in mind as well as in body.

All the carefully-laid plans went out the window when Dan Pastorini got hurt before the season even started. The Raiders were stuck with Jim Plunkett, a retread who had not played good football in five years. Everyone wrote Oakland off.

But Al Davis, working with his head coach, Tom Flores, nursed Jim Plunkett along slowly. They built up his confidence. In the beginning, they gave him a small offensive game plan to work with. They built the game plan up slowly, never giving him more than they thought he could handle. They knew they would never get a truckload of points with Plunkett at quarterback. They just wanted to get a few, and not make the kind of mistakes that would give the ball away in bad field position too often. They placed total reliance on the team's strong defense. If the defensive boys weren't overtaxed, if they didn't have to stay on the field too long, if they didn't have to start almost every defensive series backed up against their own goal line, they could perform. As the season wore on, it became increasingly evident that the new Raider plan was working. The offense was scoring just enough to be competitive. And whatever the offense scored, the defense allowed less. Lester Hayes, John Matuzak, Ted Hendricks, and Rod Martin were doing a good job.

Rod Martin is a pleasant young man with a deep voice and matching chuckle. He laughs a lot and seems to enjoy himself. He especially enjoys playing football. Born on April 7, 1954 in Welch, West Virginia, he came to Los Angeles when he was 12. He made his first public athletic mark at Hamilton High School in the City of Angels. An All-City fullback who doubled as a linebacker, Martin's combination of speed and power set him above most of those he competed against. Showing his athletic versatility, Rod also played forward and center on the basketball team and long jumped and tripled jumped on the track team.

"My older brother was into basketball, and I looked up to him," Martin said. "But I thought I'd give football a try. My first year of football, which was my junior year at Hamilton, I was named All-League fullback. From then on, football was for me because I liked the awards."

Martin became a junior college All-American linebacker at Los Angeles City College in 1973. He played quarterback with Vince Evans who, like Rod, went on to USC.

"Vince was the most valuable player on offense in our state junior college title game, and I got the defensive award," Martin continued.

Ironically, Martin's home in Los Angeles is much closer to the UCLA campus than to USC. Because of that, he almost enrolled there. But he changed his mind the week before school started and decided to become a Trojan instead of a Bruin.

"It was a difficult decision," he said. "But everyone knows about USC's championship background in football. I consider myself a good player. I thought if I played at USC my pro football chances would be that much better. They've got a lot of players in the pros."

Rod was right. People do watch USC football players closely. Al Davis has said on more than one occasion that he liked ballplayers from Southern California, that he watched them closely and, when given a chance, he will always draft a Trojan with talent. Davis' feelings toward USC players could partially stem from the fact that he was an assistant coach at that university during the 1950s.

Davis saw Rod Martin start five of USC's final seven games in 1975. Rod played outside linebacker and was the outstanding player in the Trojans 20-0 victory over Texas A&M in the Liberty Bowl. He made 12 tackles, including five for losses. David Lewis, the Trojan's other outside linebacker, was also outstanding in that game. Though the Martin and Lewis linebacking combination was fun for USC fans to watch, they were hardly funny to USC's opponents.

Rod Martin intercepts for the Raiders in Super Bowl XV.

True to his word, Al Davis picked USC's Rod Martin in the 1977 draft. Even if he was light for an NFL linebacker at 210 pounds, Davis liked his speed and quickness.

"We drafted Rodney in the 12th round," Davis said, "but we were loaded in 1977. We had just come off our first Super Bowl victory and, even though he did everything we asked of him, and we loved his 4.7 speed, we had to cut him. The 49ers picked him up, but they let him go."

Disappointed, but not beaten, Martin talked to people with several clubs. The Kansas City Chiefs, the Chicago Bears, and the Tampa Bay Buccaneers worked him out. Each told him to leave his number, they'd get back to him.

The 1977 season wore on. No one contacted Rod. Still, he worked out regularly. He stayed in as good a shape as possible, figuring the call that would get him back into football would come at any time. When it did come, he wanted to be ready. He ran every day on the beach. He worked with weights as he tried to build himself up a bit. Rod realized that one of the problems he was running into was weight prejudice. Pro teams thought he was too light to play linebacker at 210.

The call he was expecting came from the Raiders late in the 1977 season. Linebacker Phil Villapiano had gotten hurt, and the Raiders needed a linebacker quickly. Suddenly, Rod didn't look so small. For his part, Rod was happy to be hired back where he had started.

In 1980, the Oakland defense was designed with John Matuzak, at 6-foot-8 and 280 pounds, and Ted Hendricks, at 6-foot-7, 225 pounds, playing on the same side. Teams tended to stay away from their area. Thus, much work and responsibility went to Rod's side.

The work and responsibility piled up for Rod as Super Bowl XV approached. He knew that the Eagles, like most teams, would try to load up against his side of the defense. It made sense. Pro football coaches like to play the percentages, do things that figure to turn out right more times than they figure to turn out wrong. Hendricks had been all-pro linebacker for more than ten years. Rod Martin was a no-name.

Going into the game, the Eagles were a three-point favorite. The oddsmaker chose to ignore the AFC's Super Bowl dominance and instead focused on Philadelphia's 10-7 victory over the Raiders during the regular season. That game had been in Philadelphia and, though the Eagles had won that day, there was no clear-cut edge in play.

In Super Bowl XV, the Eagles took the opening kick off. Three plays into the game, quarterback Ron Jaworski decided to throw a pass. He completed it to Rod Martin, who, unfortunately for Jaworski, played for the Raiders. Martin picked the pass out of the air on the Eagle 47 and ran it down to the 30. Seven plays later, speedy wide receiver Cliff Branch caught a two-yard pass from Jim Plunkett, and the Raiders led 7-0.

Soon they led 14-0. With the ball on the Raider 20, third down and four yards to go, Plunkett moved toward the line of scrimmage as if he were going to run the ball. Herman Edwards, the Eagles' defensive back, was so sure that he was going to scramble that, after looking at running back Kenny King, who was in the pass pattern, and seeing him tucked along the sideline, he moved up quickly to cut Plunkett off. Suddenly, Jim stopped running and threw a short pass to the wide-open King. The former Oklahoma fullback, who could run 100 yards in 9.5 seconds, outran everyone to the goal line. A field goal with five minutes left in the half was the total Eagle scoring output in the first half.

If the team from Philadelphia expected things to get better in the second half, they quickly found out they were mistaken. The Raiders came out of their dressing room ready to eat the Eagles alive. In five plays, their lead soared to 18 points. Two long passes did most of the damage. Plunkett completed a 32-yard pass to wide receiver Bob Chandler. He followed with a 29-yard scoring toss to Cliff Branch. Branch made a great play in outfighting Philadelphia cornerback Roynell Young for the underthrown ball.

It was the Eagle's ball and, once again, Jaworski hit Rod Martin. This time, it really hurt. The Eagles were driving. A touchdown here, and it was still a ballgame. But Martin's catch on the Raider 34 blunted the Eagle drive and led to a Raider field goal, which upped their lead to 24-3.

The fourth quarter saw the Eagles score a touchdown, and the Raiders countered with a field goal, making the final score 27-10. Also in the fourth quarter, Ron Jaworski hit Rod Martin in the flat with another perfect pass.

Though Jim Plunkett won the game's MVP award, there is little doubt that the Raiders couldn't have won without Rod Martin's excellent work. His interceptions not only led directly to numerous Oakland points, but his overall play kept the Philadelphians off balance all day. If his comeback story seems pale next to Plunkett's, those who know the man from Los Angeles realize how much courage he showed in sticking it out. And if the honors didn't pour in for Rod as they did for Plunkett, at least he was getting some recognition. It was like high school, with awards coming his way. The most prestigious came from the Citizens Savings Bank Foundation, which has been awarding athletic excellence for nearly half a century. In one afternoon, the man who had been cut twice, and had been told numerous times, "Don't call us, we'll call you," won lasting fame as a star of Super Bowl XV.